Stories

WITH A MESSAGE

for the

secondary school

Helping you deal with difficult issues

RACHEL ADAMS

ACKNOWLEDGEMENTS

I would like to thank my family for their patience and support when I had my writing head on, and the lovely teachers who were kind enough to trial my stories with their classes.

I would also like to thank Megan Crowe and the rest of the team at LDA for all their support in getting this book to print, and Robin Lawrie for his hard work on the illustrations.

Stories with a message for the secondary school

ISBN: 978-1-85503-590-4

© Rachel Adams 2015

Illustrations by Robin Lawrie

This edition published 2015

10 9 8 7 6 5 4 3 2 1

Printed in the UK by Page Bros (Norwich) Ltd

Designed and typeset by Andy Wilson for Green Desert Ltd

LDA, 2 Gregory Street, Hyde, Cheshire, SK14 4HR

www.ldalearning.com

CONTENTS

✧ Gender identity and sexuality

⬡ Violence and anti-social behaviour

☆ Anxiety, depression, self-harm and suicide

ABOUT THIS BOOK

I was working in a primary school when I first realised that a subtle approach can be useful when tackling difficult social and emotional issues with pupils. We've all encountered students who can take offence at the slightest hint of criticism or who find it hard to speak up. If we can use a story to get a message across to a troubled student (even without them realising this is why they are reading it) then we can avoid confrontation, embarrassment and other problems that a more direct approach can sometimes create.

I now work in a secondary school and witness daily the transition from child to young adult and all the teen angst that goes with this change. Today's young people often lead complicated lives and have much to deal with. *Stories with a message* is the indirect approach to tackling difficult issues that some students need. It gives them no chance to rebel against the 'injustice' of being told off or walk away shrugging their shoulders. Instead, they are given the opportunity to step off the treadmill, consider the meaning of the story and absorb the relevance it has to their own lives.

Each of the following stories is designed to cover at least one area of concern commonly identified in secondary schools in a subtle story format and is reinforced with accompanying discussion questions. These can be used as a starting point for opening further discussion and debate or as a written exercise on an individual, group or whole-class level. They are ideal for use in PSHE lessons and are also a great way to reinforce a particular message during detention or isolation.

The ultimate aim of this resource is to persuade students to consider those around them and the situations in which they might find themselves. It encourages a deeper understanding of cause and effect, right and wrong, and reward and consequence. The questions at the end of each story also allow you to gain an interesting insight into the thoughts and emotions of individual students.

You're mine

"Why were you talking to her?" Ellie asked suspiciously when she finally had the opportunity to speak to Neil. Neil cast his eyes skyward in exasperation at Ellie's sulky question.

"I grew up with Deana, we're just friends!" It took Neil all of his patience to maintain his calm exterior when what he really wanted to say was 'Back off!'. Ellie could be so possessive. "Anyway," he continued, "I promised I would help her with her homework tonight." Neil quickly walked away before he heard any objections.

Later that day, Neil caught up with his friends. They began to tease him as soon as he drew near.

"Where's Ellie? She *never* lets you out on your own," Shaun joked.

"Knock it off, Shaun!" Neil was not in the mood.

Shaun wasn't going to let it drop though; it was so rare to see his friend without his constant shadow. He continued making jokes until Neil finally snapped.

"Look, what exactly are you getting at?" Neil could feel his hands clenching into fists.

"Okay, calm down. It's just that we've all had it in the neck from your girlfriend. She wants to know where you are, who you're with, what you're doing..." Shaun was in full flow until James interrupted him.

"...shoe size, what you had for breakfast, total time taken on the toilet today..." James laughingly carried on from where Shaun left off until he caught sight of Neil's face.
He let his sentence trail off.

Neil had had enough. He knew his friends meant no harm and were just making light of it all, but deep down he knew that he couldn't put up with Ellie much longer. They had been going out with each other for two months and Ellie now classed him as her own personal property. This was not healthy.

That evening, Neil was walking home from Deana's house. He realised that for the first time in two months he felt relaxed. He had really enjoyed the company of his friend while he had helped her with her homework. Deana was fun to talk to, always ready with an amusing story and there was absolutely no pressure over anything.

Just as he reached the turning up to his house he heard footsteps. As he turned, he saw Ellie behind him and realised that she'd followed him home. She'd been waiting for him to come out of Deana's house. This was ridiculous. He could sense her eyes boring into the side of his head as he stood waiting for her to catch up.

2

"Fancy inviting me in?" Ellie was slightly out of breath from her race to catch up with him.

At that moment, Neil made a decision. At that moment, he realised that things had to change.

"No, sorry. I'm busy now."

"Well, what about tomorrow?" Ellie was certainly persistent.

"Actually, I might be permanently busy where you're concerned." Neil turned towards his house again and strode purposefully on, his sense of relief telling him that he had just done the right thing.

What do you think?

1. Why might Neil have felt that Ellie was being too possessive of his time and attention?

2. Describe how you think Ellie made Neil feel.

3. Why do you think Ellie behaved this way with Neil?

4. If you were Ellie, would you be happy for Neil to visit Deana's house on his own? Explain your answer.

5. What advice would you give to Neil and Ellie in this situation?

6. Explain why you think Shaun and James found Neil's situation with Ellie so funny.

7. Do you think Neil broke up with Ellie in the right way? Describe what he could have done differently.

8. Do you have any sympathy for Ellie at the end of the story? Explain your answer.

9. Do you think Ellie will behave differently with future boyfriends? Explain your answer.

10. Describe the consequences for Ellie if she continues to behave like this in future relationships.

Don't look at me!

Friday morning. At last! It had been a long week.

Imogen looked critically at the tired reflection staring back at her from the mirror as she brushed her hair. She knew she was no oil painting, but the permanent eruptions all over her face had reached volcanic proportions. Raised, painful, yellow-headed spots reddened her entire face. Imogen likened herself to a swamp creature. To make it worse, the latest concoction from the chemist had dried her skin and now she had to contend with rough flakiness as well as mini Mount Etnas. Imogen was already having a bad day and she could tell that it was not going to improve any time soon.

She could feel the sun's rays on her face as she trudged up the hill to school and enjoyed their momentary warmth before the sun disappeared behind another cloud. The doctor had told her that the sun would work wonders for her skin and she was living in hope that the forthcoming summer holidays would signal an end to her nightmare.

She quietly ate her sandwiches apart from the others at lunchtime, without drawing attention to herself. She subconsciously began to pull down a curtain of hair over the side of her face in a bid to hide her skin.

Just as she was packing up her lunchbox with the remains of her crusts and her empty crisp packet, she became aware of a pair of feet standing right in front of her. She shyly looked up into the face of a new boy who had just started in her maths class.

"Hi, I thought it was you. What are you doing on your own?" Guy spoke with such ease to her and yet she found herself rooted to the spot, waiting for the first hurtful remark about her skin. It was bound to come next.

When she didn't answer, Guy cleared his throat and tried again.

"Hello? Earth calling Planet Vacant? Is anyone there?" He was smiling, so Imogen guessed he didn't mean to be rude.

"Hello," she said warily, afraid that he might suddenly say something about her skin that would spoil the moment, as so many in her class already had.

"So can I sit down, or what?" Guy didn't wait for a reply. He sat down heavily on the chair to her side and began to unwrap his baguette. Glancing sideways occasionally, a confused Imogen was left to wonder why this tall, dark, handsome stranger was bothering with her at all. He seemed so out of her league. She didn't speak to him as she hadn't a hope of getting a sensible answer when he was demolishing his baguette like he hadn't eaten in months. She just sat drinking the last of her juice, wanting to stay and talk but hating the possibility that if she did, he would just get up and walk away. She'd feel so stupid.

"Sorry about that, I was starving!" Guy was wiping crumbs off his chin with the back of his hand and had turned to look at her intensely, seemingly unaware of her mixed emotions.

Instead of getting up and walking away, Guy started to chat and before long they were engrossed in conversation. Imogen felt more comfortable than she had for a very long time and even forgot about her spots. He didn't seem to notice them, so why should she?

At the end of the best lunch ever, Guy stood up to leave but promised to meet her there again tomorrow.

As they got to know each other better over their lunch breaks, Guy confided that he had had terrible acne until fairly recently, but that in his last school he'd had some really good mates so they hadn't made a fuss about it. And when they'd started getting spots too, it hadn't altered the way he saw them.

Of course, Guy's friendship was never going to change what others thought, but it certainly gave Imogen some much-needed confidence. He had even said that she shouldn't worry because she was lovely.

Guy had told her she was lovely!

Weeks later, Imogen was walking to her next lesson after yet another enjoyable lunchtime spent with Guy. She hardly registered the group of girls on the stairway as she passed them on her way to class.

"Oi! I thought the plague died out years ago!" shouted one particularly spiteful individual with a face like a chewed toffee.

Surprisingly, Imogen didn't feel hurt or upset. She stood calmly and looked at the girl for a few moments. Imogen asked herself why it was that the worst offenders in the teasing stakes had no right to feel better about their own appearance than she did about hers. She supposed that they probably had issues with their own appearance and just needed to feel superior.

She didn't want to dignify the remark with a reply, but hoped the withering look she gave was enough. She walked on, leaving the girl and her friends looking embarrassed behind her.

Imogen didn't care.

Imogen was lovely.

© Rachel Adams 2015   *Stories with a message for the secondary school*   LDA   Permission to photocopy

What do you think?

1. At the start of the story, Imogen tried to hide away because of her skin. How do you think she could have dealt with the situation differently?

2. Describe an incident that has happened to you or someone you know where hurtful remarks have been made. How did you/they cope with the situation?

3. How can acne affect someone physically and emotionally?

4. If your friend had acne, how do you think you could try to help them without causing offence?

5. What could be done to include someone in your class who appeared to be on their own a lot?

6. Why do you think people try to make others feel bad about themselves by making nasty comments?

7. How would you feel if you had to endure constant teasing?

8. List some reasons why you think Imogen might be reluctant to do anything about the way others treat her.

9. Do you think Imogen would tease any of her classmates who have been cruel to her if they got acne? Explain your answer.

10. *People in glass houses shouldn't throw stones.*

    Explain what you think this phrase means in relation to this story.

Who's the coward?

In the stand-off with Doug, Mark could feel his anger welling up as if it was a physical object pushing its way up into the back of his throat. He could feel his heart hammering in his chest and hear it pounding in his ears as his hands balled into fists. Doug was still smirking, standing there as if he had done nothing wrong, insensitive to the feelings of his victim and cheered on by the surrounding ill-mannered individuals he chose to call friends.

Mark had done nothing to deserve the comment. It had been uncalled for and hurtful and now, faced with a baying crowd of witnesses, he felt powerless to do anything about it. What he wanted to do was fight back and hit Doug with the hardest punch he could imagine.

"Aw, look at the baby! Just standing there like a rabbit caught in the headlights! What's the matter, coward? Too scared to fight back?" Doug sneered as he poked his finger into Mark's chest. The crowd fell silent, waiting for Mark's next move.

Standing practically nose to nose with Doug, Mark was forced to look directly into the cold eyes of the vile individual in front of him. It suddenly dawned on him that retaliation was what Doug and his mates wanted. They wanted to be entertained; this was their sport. Mark could feel his anger dissolve as he stood and studied the twisted features of the boy before him. The cruel expression on Doug's face only added to his ugly exterior.

In those few moments, Mark experienced a sense of realisation that would stay with him for years to come. He asked himself one important question: *why should I get myself into trouble by lashing out at someone who is more to be pitied than feared?*

Mark had never before, in all the time that Doug had bullied him, actually felt this powerful. The anger that had threatened to overspill subsided. He had found the strength to bring his anger under control without creating consequences for himself. He was the powerful one. He knew that such self-control took more strength than it could ever have taken Doug to surround himself with his army of followers and pick on one lone boy.

Mark started to laugh. He felt no fear, no anger. He was in control and he liked it. He laughed with relief as he realised that Doug actually looked quite funny with his put-on menace and silly expressions. All his bravado was for show in front of his sad little mates; without them, he would be nothing.

Mark took a step closer to Doug. Doug backed away slightly.

"Up close, mate, your breath really stinks. You should get yourself some mints or something." Mark's voice was firm and just loud enough for the group to hear.

Mark started to laugh again as a shocked Doug and his gang stood for a moment, their jaws hanging. Doug had gone red in the face. Mark couldn't work out if it was through embarrassment or rage but at that moment, he didn't really care. He could see his support teacher coming down the corridor behind their heads to look for him. He was ten minutes late for class and Mr Smith was worried about him.

Mark was so glad he had confided in Mr Smith yesterday. All through primary school and into secondary, Doug and his mates had frightened him into silence. Mr Smith had helped him to see that it needn't be like that. This would be a new start.

"Head's office at break!" Mr Smith pointed to Doug and his friends. "Mark, with me now, you're late!"

Walking with Mr Smith down the corridor, Mark felt six feet tall.

"Thanks sir!" he said quietly.

"You're welcome," Mr Smith replied.

What do you think?

1. Have you ever met anyone like Doug? Describe what you thought of them.

2. Why do you think people like Doug bully others? Consider personal circumstances and personalities.

3. What behaviour would you class as bullying?

4. What course of action would you take if you were the victim of bullying?

5. What concerns would you have about telling someone that you were being bullied?

6. What part did Mr Smith play in helping Mark to overcome his fear of the bullies?

7. What do you think would have happened next if Mr Smith had not arrived? Explain your answer.

8. How do you think Doug and Mark will behave towards each other from now on?

9. What would make you feel safer in school if you were being bullied?

10. Write either a poem or a diary entry from the perspective of a victim of bullying. The poem doesn't need to rhyme but it has to be descriptive.

© Rachel Adams 2015 *Stories with a message for the secondary school* LDA Permission to photocopy

Far too busy for homework

It was far too nice to stay in and do homework. Dawn had arranged to meet Ellie by the chip shop at five o' clock. She changed out of her stifling school uniform and quickly side-stepped her mum on the stairs, ignoring her nagging. She tripped out of the door into the waiting sunshine and didn't look back. She could just imagine her mum ranting and raving about her not doing her homework again and moaning about how 'irresponsible' she was being or how she needed to 'grow up' or something. Dawn couldn't be bothered with it.

But her mum was not ranting and raving. She only felt sad. She watched as her defiant daughter ran down the garden path and out onto the street as if she didn't have a care in the world, her wind-tossed hair bouncing about on her shoulders as she went. Mum remembered a time when she had also felt that freedom and had possessed that same couldn't-care-less attitude. She sighed and returned inside. She had given up on saying anything to Dawn within a few weeks of the new school year. She couldn't understand what had happened to her daughter; it was as if she hardly knew her anymore.

The following day, after the third lunchtime detention she'd received for not handing in her homework, Dawn made her way to maths. She suddenly remembered that she had been given homework for that too.

"Damn it!" Dawn muttered as she quickly looked in her planner to see when the homework had been due in. *Today*. Mr Jalloh would be cross with her too, but it was too late to bunk off now; he had already seen her. She'd have to admit that she hadn't done her maths homework yet again.

Surprisingly, he seemed only a little annoyed and allowed her to do it at the end of the lesson while the rest of the class were still completing the work that she had already finished. She was bright and, as with most subjects, maths was no problem to her. She smiled to herself when she thought of how her friend Ellie always had to work extra hard in lessons and needed extra tuition after school for a couple of subjects. Unlike Ellie, Dawn was in the top set for everything.

It was the last day of the school year before Dawn finally realised that all her unfinished homework and assessments had taken their toll. Her heart sank when she opened her report on her way home from school. Her results averages had been brought down by the lack of marks for all the homework she had failed to complete and she had been dropped to second set in all her subjects. It was there in black and white and there was nothing she could do about it.

Dawn was upset and deep in thought when an animated Ellie caught up with her. They walked part of the way home together, Ellie chatting excitedly about how her report was the best ever and how happy her mum would be that she was being put up a set in all her subjects. Dawn could hardly speak; she was too worried about the prospect of handing her mum the worst end-of-year report she had ever had. She felt too ashamed to let on to Ellie how badly she had done. She wanted to cry.

Later, her mum read the report and carefully slipped it back inside its envelope. Dawn had expected her to be mortified, to yell and ask her what had happened.

She didn't.

Dawn hoped that her mum would comfort her and sympathise with her and become angry with school because such a dreadful report was unfair.

She didn't.

Dawn expected fighting talk from her mum; surely she would promise to go into school and get the matter cleared up so she could move back up to the top set.

She didn't.

Instead, she quietly left the room with one question hanging in the air.

"What did you expect, Dawn?"

What do you think?

1. Why do you think teachers set homework?

2. Consider how much homework you get in a week. How do you manage to organise your time in order to get it all done and still have some free time?

3. If you had been given too much homework to be able to complete it all in time what would you do about it?

4. Describe what influences your attitude towards doing your homework.

5. Dawn considers herself to be clever. How do you think this has influenced her attitude towards her homework?

6. What practical and emotional consequences have Dawn's attitude towards her homework eventually had on her?

7. Describe how you think Mum feels about her daughter in the story.

8. Do you think Mum should have tried harder to tell Dawn about the consequences of not doing her homework? Explain your answer.

9. Describe how you think Dawn feels about her friend Ellie throughout the story.

10. Do you think it is too late for Dawn to put matters right at school? Describe what you think she could do to help her situation when she returns to school after the summer holiday.

Let me stay in bed, Mum!

"You're going to be late. Get yourself up, now!" Mum's not-so-gentle tones drifted up the stairs and fell on deaf ears as Shona lay in bed; warm and cosy, cocooned inside her lavender-scented duvet. She had no intention of getting up. Shona knew her mum was a soft touch. She'd only have to tell her that she was feeling ill and give a little cough as she said it and Mum would run around getting someone to cover for her at work. The rest of the day would then consist of them sitting together on the sofa watching rubbish daytime TV and drinking tea until Dad got home.

"Mum," Shona managed to croak pathetically as her mum poked her head around the bedroom door. "I feel ill again." Shona gave a little cough to add emphasis and awaited her mum's reaction.

"Shona, what's wrong? Do you have a temperature? Perhaps I should call the doctor; there's flu about at the moment. But I'd better call work first. Where's that thermometer?" Mum was still muttering halfway down the stairs. Shona could twist her mum around her little finger and knew she had won when the worried expression appeared and the dithering started. Happy days! Shona snuggled back down into the depths of her duvet and went back to sleep.

School the following day was difficult. After each absence it got harder and harder to understand the work she'd missed and her friends seemed a little more distant towards her. It was obvious that she was getting more and more behind the rest of her class in all of her subjects. The pace of the schoolwork had picked up and on top of that, the maths teacher wanted her to use her lunch break to do the assessment she thought she'd avoided yesterday. Shona was not happy, but she was sure she could wangle a few more days out of her mum if necessary.

That evening, Shona noticed that Mum was quieter than usual. She had been talking to Dad in hushed tones in the kitchen for ages since he had arrived home. Mum had been in line for a promotion last year, but Shona thought she'd heard her saying something about a meeting with her boss who had suggested she might prefer another job. Dad had chipped in something about not being able to afford the mortgage. Shona wasn't sure what was going on.

After she'd finished her dinner, Shona asked her mum what was wrong.

"Oh, it's nothing really," Mum sighed. "My boss had a word with me this morning about the number of days I've had to ask him to get cover for me. They know you're ill and we all understand that you can't help that. If they can't provide cover for when I have to be off to look after you, well, that's their problem, isn't it? You'll always come first in my life, darling. The client I'd got the meeting with wasn't happy about having to reschedule again, that's all." She sighed again. "It'll all blow over, I'm sure. It'll be fine. Anyway, let's have a cup of tea!"

Mum was a little too quick to change the subject and her brow was still furrowed. Shona noticed Dad watching Mum as she got up from the table to put the kettle on. He had been quiet all evening.

Shona wasn't convinced that it would all blow over. Nor was she convinced that it would be fine.

What do you think?

1. Have you ever been tempted to pretend to be ill to stay off from school? Explain why or why not.

2. Why do you think some people choose to get out of going to school?

3. How would you feel about a friend you suspected of lying to avoid going to school? Explain your answer.

4. How do you think Shona has felt about going back to school since she started to avoid it?

5. How do you think Shona's attitude towards returning to school might change now she knows about Mum's difficulties at work?

6. How do you think Shona's absences will have impacted her schoolwork and friendships?

7. What could be done to help Shona get back into the routine of going to school? Explain who you think would be the best people to help.

8. List some possible long-term consequences of Shona's actions. Consider her education and her relationships with her friends and family.

9. Have you ever felt uncomfortable when there have been worrying consequences as a result of your own actions? If so, describe the circumstances.

10. Write an ending for the story in which Shona does what you consider to be the right thing.

© Rachel Adams 2015 *Stories with a message for the secondary school* LDA Permission to photocopy

Who's that girl?

The attic was hot and stuffy. It even *smelt* warm. Specks of dust escaped into the stale air as Danny pulled out box after dusty box.

Danny was still in a mood with his dad. He understood that Dad had to find work and he understood that he had to move to find it. What he was having difficulty with was the fact that he was expecting them all to go with him. It would mean leaving behind everyone he cared about: friends, family, Emily from number 32. It just wasn't fair. Dad should be the one to move and leave them all at home. He could find a bedsit to stay in during the week. He could send money to Mum and come home at weekends. That way, none of them would have to move, they wouldn't have to sell the house and Danny wouldn't be getting filthy dirty sorting out a lifetime's worth of junk in an overstuffed attic. He was not happy!

Dad had always been a mystery to Danny. He was a good dad, though he was a little miserable at times, but Danny thought he was too protective, too fussy – and that was before the added stress of losing his job as well. Danny resented Dad for never allowing him enough freedom. There were always arguments whenever he asked if he could go to see a friend. He hadn't dared mention that he'd started seeing Emily from number 32; Dad would hit the roof! Since he had lost his job, their already uncomfortable relationship had got even worse.

"Damn it! Damn it! Damn it!" Danny cursed as he hopped about on one leg. He had just dropped a little wooden chest on his foot and the photographs it had contained were now strewn across the attic floor.

"What on earth are you doing up there?" Dad's voice boomed up through the attic hatch and Danny could hear him getting closer.

"I just dropped something on my foot. I'm okay." Danny hoped that Dad would just stay where he was, but of course that wasn't a possibility when there was an excuse to fuss.

"Is it broken? Are you hurt? Let me look at it." Dad was up the attic ladder in a flash.

"Dad, I'm fine. Leave it. Honestly, it's fine now," Danny whined at his dad in an effort to avoid an unnecessary trip to the local hospital's casualty department. When he didn't hear the fussing he was expecting, Danny looked over to see that Dad had picked up a handful of the spilled photographs from the floor and had sat down heavily on a nearby suitcase. He was completely silent, completely still.

Danny went and stood to look over his dad's shoulder. The photos were of a girl that Danny had never seen before. She was really pretty.

Like Emily from number 32, Danny thought. The girl had dark shoulder-length hair and big blue eyes. She was standing by a much younger version of his dad. The photos were obviously pre-Mum and Danny assumed that she was one of his dad's old girlfriends.

Never one to miss an opportunity, Danny started teasing his dad, blackmailing him for the money he needed for some new trainers he wanted and threatening to tell Mum he'd caught him ogling photos of his ex-girlfriend in the attic. Danny was having a whale of a time.

"Shut up, Danny!" Dad's voice was quiet and sharp. Danny was caught off guard and looked quickly at his dad's face. He was crying silent tears, his hands were shaking and his shoulders were heaving with the effort of suppressing his sobs. The sight shocked Danny.

"She's my sister." Dad stood up and quickly cleared the photos back into the box. As he stepped onto the ladder to go back down, he gently picked up the box to take it with him. Danny was confused. His dad only had one sister and she had died last year. It couldn't be Auntie Claire with all the problems she had. What was all this about? He could no longer settle to anything in the attic and decided to go down and find Mum. She'd know what Dad was talking about. He picked up a photo Dad had missed on the way down.

He found Mum staring out of the kitchen window. Dad's retreating back was disappearing into the garden shed. He had the wooden box under his arm.

"What's up with him now? He's so moody. I was only joking and he—" Danny didn't finish. He could tell from Mum's silence that there was something very wrong.

"The photos you found were of his sister, your Auntie Claire," Mum sighed. Danny felt like he'd been slapped in the face.

"I know it's hard to believe. She'd been so ill for such a long time. The accident altered everything. Your dad wants to remember the Claire you saw in the photos, but she died fifteen years ago when she stepped in front of a car without looking. It happened before you were born. They'd had a row and Claire was cross with your dad. She walked off in a temper and didn't see the car coming. Your dad saw it all. He's never forgiven himself."

Danny had never thought to ask about Auntie Claire's condition. He had assumed she'd always been that way. How would he feel if he had seen his sister being run over? He shuddered. Why had no-one told him before?

"They were inseparable when they were growing up – like two peas in a pod, according to your nan," Mum continued. She looked sadly at Danny. "It's not your fault, love. He just can't deal with it all at the moment." Mum sighed. "Anyway, that attic won't clear itself."

She pushed past him to go up to the attic armed with a roll of bin bags, leaving Danny in the kitchen. He stared at the photo in his hand. He had just discovered an auntie he never knew existed. There she was, smiling up at him. The face of the pretty girl in the photo was so familiar. She had the same eyes and the same happy expression as his younger dad in the photo beside her. The girl in the photo was tanned and healthy in a swimming costume, climbing rocks by the sea, sharing a joke with Dad, smiling.

The image he had of Auntie Claire before she died last year was very different. The accident had altered her facial features beyond recognition. The beautiful blue eyes were blind and expressionless, the bright smile had been replaced by a gaping mouth. The body that had once been able to climb rocks had become a shapeless form slumped in a wheelchair. Worst of all, Danny realised guiltily, was the fact that she had obviously had a bubbly personality once, yet to him she had barely existed. Danny found himself feeling tearful. He had never thought of his Auntie Claire as anything other than being looked after in a home, being visited daily by his nan and dad. When she died he had hardly shed a tear. He had assumed that it was good she was no longer suffering.

He had never truly understood what went on in his dad's head, but perhaps now he was beginning to.

What do you think?

1. Describe how you think Dad's family has dealt with the issues surrounding Claire's accident. Do you think they could have dealt with the situation in a better way?

2. Explain why you think the family didn't discuss Claire's accident with Danny. Do you think they should have done?

3. Do you think Danny might regret the way he has behaved towards his dad in the past now he knows about Claire? Explain your answer.

4. How do you think Danny and his dad could improve their relationship?

5. What effect do you think Claire's accident had on Dad's relationship with the rest of his family?

6. When someone suffers a serious brain injury, it can alter them mentally and physically. How could you try to support a friend who witnesses such a transformation?

7. How do you think Dad feels about having to move his family away from the area for his new job?

8. If you had to move, what concerns would you have and what would you miss the most?

9. How do you think Dad and the rest of the family could make moving house easier for each other?

10. Imagine that Danny wants to talk to Dad about what he has discovered. Write a script of the conversation they might have. Consider when the right moment would be for them to have this conversation.

I'm just as clever

"Lewis, where is your homework? I even wrote it down in your homework diary for you. You have absolutely no excuse." Mr Peel's frustration was written all over his face. "You know this is going to mean lunchtime detention again!"

"No change there, then," Lewis muttered under his breath. Ever since he could remember it had always been the same; it never got any easier. No-one understood.

"Take this note to detention with you and hand it to Mrs Walker." Mr Peel slapped a note on the desk in front of Lewis as the bell rang for morning break. "If you are going to achieve anything in this school, you will have to take your work more seriously. This can't go on, Lewis. Your physics assessment is well overdue."

"Yeah, I'll just add it to the list. Thanks for that!" Lewis grabbed the note and his bag and left Mr Peel looking after his retreating back.

Outside, Lewis was immediately sorry for his aggressive tone of voice and the way he had barged past Mr Peel. He would have to find him later to apologise. The poor man was only trying to tell him what he already knew.

"Oi, thicko! Detention again? You must love Mrs Walker, you're always in there! You've got a thing about grey hair and glasses, admit it!" Asim, his friend since primary school, said as he caught up with him. He was the last person Lewis wanted to bump into; he could be such a wind-up merchant.

"Leave it out, Asim, I'm not in the mood," Lewis said as he quickened his pace, but Asim kept up with him as he walked towards the tuck shop.

"I got full marks in that English assessment last week. I heard you'll have to do it again. Shame!" Asim's sarcasm was barely concealed by his cheeky grin. Lewis chose to ignore him.

Seeing no reaction from his friend, Asim couldn't resist continuing his teasing.

"And didn't you get three out of twenty in that history assessment too, thicko?"

That was the last straw.

Lewis stopped in his tracks. He leaned menacingly towards Asim.

"I am not thick!" he shouted at the top of his voice.

"Blimey, I was just saying! You need help, you do!" Asim shouted over his shoulder as he quickly ran ahead into the tuck shop.

Perhaps I do, Lewis thought. He could usually tolerate Asim's stupid sense of humour but he was sick and tired of the stupid comments, the detentions for not doing homework that seemed impossible, the low grades and the way he was feeling about himself. He was constantly exhausted by his own attempts to hide his difficulties from others. Asim's relentless jibes were the last straw. He had had enough.

After two more fruitless lessons trying to copy words off a whiteboard, he arrived in the detention room. He waited patiently for Mr Rai to finish talking to Mrs Walker before handing her the note. Lewis remembered that Mr Rai was Head of Learning Support and in charge of providing extra support for students who needed more help with their schoolwork. He felt suddenly unsure of himself, caught between wanting to ask for help and not wanting to appear stupid in front of the others in detention.

"S— s— sir?" Lewis stammered nervously, his cheeks reddening.

"Yes?" Mr Rai turned to look at Lewis.

Lewis had committed himself to saying something. It was too late to stop now, but he still couldn't face saying it in front of everyone else.

"I— er— I— um— I wondered if I could talk to you later." Lewis felt silly. The words wouldn't come to him easily; his mind simply refused to co-operate.

"Of course. I could see you in my classroom after school if that's any good?" Mr Rai said. Lewis thought he seemed okay.

"Thanks, sir." Lewis felt proud of himself for saying something as he took his seat.

Two months later, Lewis felt like a different person as he sat with his friends in the lunch hall explaining why he had started using a laptop for his schoolwork. Lewis recounted his meeting with Mr Rai that day. Lewis had told him about the way the words on pages and whiteboards moved about as he tried to read them. He told his friends that he had shown Mr Rai his exercise books covered in his teachers' red pen markings, pointing out mistakes in his writing and spelling.

"So, what did he do to help you?" Keisha sat forward with interest.

"Within a month, Mr Rai had met with Dad to tell him he thought I might have dyslexia. It's a disorder that involves having difficulty with learning to read or interpret words, letters and symbols. It doesn't affect intelligence, just the way you can process and express words." Lewis paused.

"So you're not really thick, then?" Asim chipped in cheekily.

"Asim!" There was a chorus of disapproval from the rest of Lewis' friends around the table.

"No, it's okay, really. If I hadn't been so angry with Asim that day, I might never have gone to Mr Rai. Thanks, mate!" Lewis slapped Asim on the back, a little too hard.

"You're welcome!" Asim spluttered. He considered Lewis to be his best friend; they were like brothers. He hadn't realised that his banter could have had such an impact.

"Anyway, Dad agreed to me being screened and that confirmed that I'm dyslexic. Mr Rai said it was probably behind all the problems I'd ever had in school. At least I know it has a name! Actually, I've looked it up on the internet. There are loads of celebrities with dyslexia and they don't seem any different to me. It certainly hasn't got in the way of them doing well for themselves. Mr Rai arranged for me to have a laptop to do my work on. He also found out that I can read better on coloured paper. My best colour is yellow. He's given me a clear piece of yellow plastic to put over pages in my books to help me read those too. It really helps to stop the letters look like they're moving about on the page." Lewis was feeling good about himself as he looked around the table at his friends.

Raising his voice deliberately, he decided to inform them all that he got full marks for his physics assessment yesterday. He looked squarely at Asim as he said it. Asim shrugged his shoulders and gave a wry smile. He had only got thirteen out of twenty for that one but he couldn't have felt prouder of his friend.

What do you think?

1. Describe what you know about dyslexia.

2. Lewis says about his dyslexia 'at least I know it has a name'. Why do you think he seems relieved by this?

3. Would you have expected any of Lewis' teachers to notice that he was having problems with his schoolwork? Explain your answer.

4. Why do you think Lewis didn't discuss his difficulties with anyone or ask for help sooner?

5. If someone you knew was experiencing difficulties with their schoolwork, who could they turn to for help?

6. How would you react if you or a friend was being teased about schoolwork or learning difficulties?

7. How would you expect others to treat you if you were dyslexic? Explain your answer.

8. Describe the impression you have of Lewis and Asim's friendship throughout the story. How do you think Asim feels now he knows that Lewis is dyslexic?

9. Imagine that you are unable to complete a piece of work because you don't understand what to do. Describe a sensible solution to the problem.

10. Describe some immediate and future consequences for someone who does not speak up about any difficulties they are having with their schoolwork.

Let me out before I breathe in

The heat was unbearable. The computers had been on all day and despite the blinds being pulled down to shut out the burning rays of the summer sunshine, the stifling atmosphere in the IT room was oppressive. Breathing in warm air was one thing, but the stench of someone else's body odour was just too much for Belinda.

"Someone needs to shower when they get home!" Belinda declared to anyone who was prepared to listen. No-one answered her; there was little point. The class kept their heads down, choosing to ignore her.

"It's worse than onions – a sort of cross between shallot and garlic really!" She was on fine form today, but none of her friends were joining in.

The class always had IT after their PE lesson. During winter, no-one had noticed the aroma of changing hormones and lack of personal hygiene, but the summer had brought with it the ripening perfume of long-fermented sweat and it was definitely not pleasant.

Luckily, IT was the last lesson of the day and as soon as the bell went for home, the class stampeded out like a herd of rampaging cattle. Despite the plaintive cries of the class teacher to 'Walk! There's no hurry!', no-one was prepared to stay in the room a second longer than was absolutely necessary. Belinda was the first down the stairs.

Later, dropping her bag in the scented shade of her hallway at home, Belinda felt incredibly uncomfortable. Her shirt was sticking to her and she could feel trickles of perspiration making their way down her back.

"Mum! I'm home! What's for tea? I'm starving!" Belinda shouted down the hall to the closed kitchen door. She could hear her mum bustling about in the kitchen, clattering pans and shutting cupboard doors. Before Belinda could shout again her mum entered the hallway, just as Belinda was taking off her school shoes.

Mum stopped short, her face a mixture of confusion and horror. The words of greeting that she had been about to bestow upon her daughter stuck in her throat as the urge to gag overtook them.

"Mum, what's wrong?" Mum had gone a sickly shade of green for some reason. Belinda couldn't think why she was pulling that face.

"I'm fine, just have a shower and I'll get us a nice cold glass of lemonade and a snack for when you're out. Tea will be a while yet." Mum had regained her composure but Belinda was having none of it.

"Shower? I had one two days ago. I'm going to watch TV." Belinda had headed off towards the living room but her mum was physically blocking her path and pointing up the stairs.

"Okay, okay! I can take a hint! But it'll only be a quick shower or I'll miss my programmes!" Belinda trudged up the stairs, determined to be a maximum of two minutes.

As she removed her shirt, Belinda detected the same smell that had been so offensive in the IT room.

That smell gets everywhere, even into your clothes. I wonder who it is, Belinda thought. Suddenly, she stopped, horrified. *Oh no! It's me!*

It was the longest shower Belinda had ever had.

Tea was on the table when she finally emerged from her bedroom in an invisible cloud of deodorant and her mum's perfume.

As she walked downstairs to the kitchen only one thought was on her mind.

Why didn't anyone tell me?

What do you think?

1. Do you think anyone should have told Belinda she had a personal hygiene problem? Consider who you think the best person to tackle this difficult subject would be.

2. Write down what you think would be an appropriate way to tell Belinda.

3. If you noticed that your friend had personal hygiene problems, would you tackle the situation? If so, how?

4. List some concerns that might prevent you from broaching the subject with a friend.

5. How do you think Belinda should deal with the situation in which she now finds herself? Consider her embarrassment and worries about what others will think of her.

6. Where and by whom do you think good personal hygiene should be taught and encouraged? Explain your answer.

7. At what stage do you feel it is appropriate to start to encourage children to place more importance on their personal hygiene?

8. Create a poster advising a younger student of the ways in which they can take care of their personal hygiene.

You stink!

It had always felt good to have his own little patch of paradise in the park. It was a useful hideaway to escape to for a sneaky cigarette away from his parents. The bushes were perfect cover for him and his growing number of smoking buddies. Mum and Dad had no idea where he was or what he was doing. Just as well, because they would go ballistic if they knew!

Connor coughed and suddenly realised that he'd been smoking for six years. They had gone in a flash. He remembered how he'd first nicked his grandma's cigarettes and a lighter when he was nine and hidden them in his room for ages before he'd plucked up the courage to light up. He'd waited for the chance to go out and play and had eventually found his hiding place in the bushes. He knew that no-one could see him. He had coughed and spluttered at first and his lungs had burned for a while but, although he knew he was doing something bad, it felt good to be naughty.

From then on, he'd hidden in the park whenever he could, making his hiding place into a proper den. He had been proud of the fact that he had introduced smoking to five other kids from the estate. The youngest was only six!

Today, he didn't feel the need to hide in his den. He was older now and more self-assured, and decided to sit on the park wall. It was no fun smoking on his own though and as no-one else was about, he started to walk home, taking care to suck a mint to hide the stench of cigarettes on his breath.

"Where have you been, Connor?" Dad shouted from the sofa when he got home.

"At a mate's! So what?" Connor threw the lie at his dad as he made his way into the kitchen to make a sandwich. Dad sighed sadly at his son's attitude and turned his attention back to the TV.

The following day, Connor decided to go to the park for a quick cigarette on the way to school. He'd never had one on the way there before, but this morning he felt he just *needed* to. Dad had sat him down for what turned out to be a heated discussion about his 'attitude' late last night when Mum had come home from work. They were worried about him, apparently. Connor didn't really care.

Sitting in the fresh air in the park, Connor could hear the rustle and birdsong of the inhabitants of an overhanging tree. Inhaling the smoke into his lungs, he eventually felt ready to face the day and set off again. By the time he had reached school, it was a very different matter. He'd noticed for a while that he was getting out of breath very quickly and he couldn't play football as well as he had before he started smoking. He felt really unfit. His chest felt like it was bursting with effort and he just couldn't maintain his speed on the pitch.

Dad had frogmarched him to the doctor. Dr Jones had asked him in front of Dad if he smoked and Connor had felt his dad tense up at the mere mention of it. He was hardly going to tell the doctor the truth, was he? When he replied with a firm 'no', Dr Jones said he must have developed asthma and prescribed him an inhaler.

Connor was glad to get into the school grounds. He had to sit down on the wall for a while to catch his breath. His friend Gemma arrived just after him. He'd fancied her for ages and had made up his mind to ask her out. He thought she was bound to say yes.

"Hi, Connor!" Gemma had seen him and was making her way over to him.

"Hi!" Connor felt nervous to be so close to her. She smelled nice and every time she moved her head, her long black ponytail swished the scent of her perfume in his direction. He thought she smelled like flowers, but his sense of smell was not so good these days and he couldn't be sure.

"Gemma, do you fancy going out with me some time?" Connor felt proud of his bravery and waited, fully expecting her to accept his invitation without hesitation.

"Actually Connor, I don't want to offend you and you probably can't help it, but I really can't stand the smell of cigarettes and you always stink of them! Sorry!" With that, Gemma walked off to stand by Jay, Connor's former best friend. Jay, who had been his best mate since primary school, had deserted him when Connor had tried to make him join his growing gang of smoking buddies.

As Connor watched, Gemma and Jay turned to look at him with pity before walking into school as the bell sounded for the start of the day.

They were holding hands.

What do you think?

1. List the problems Connor now has as a result of smoking.

2. Why do you think Connor felt proud of introducing smoking to others, some of whom were much younger than himself at the time?

3. If all of your friends smoked, would you feel tempted to smoke as well? Explain your answer.

4. Why do you think Connor felt that he had to have a cigarette on his way to school?

5. How do you think Connor's parents would react if they knew about his smoking habit?

6. Do you think Gemma's words will have any effect on Connor? Explain your answer.

7. If Connor was to stop smoking immediately, do you think that he would be left with health problems or that his body would get better in time?

8. What do you know about the difficulties of trying to give up smoking? Describe some methods people use to stop smoking.

9. Describe some signs that might suggest someone is a heavy smoker.

'Sorry' is not enough

"Move! Get out of my way, will you?" Darren was like a snowplough, cutting through the mass of bodies in the corridor. He didn't see them as people with feelings, just a collection of bag-carrying obstacles that he needed to get through in order to arrive on time to his next lesson. He ignored the shouts of 'Ouch!', 'Get off!', and 'Watch it, mate!', not to mention numerous expletives.

Unfortunately, Darren had failed to notice that as he was ploughing his way down the corridor, the other students were getting increasingly larger, until one particularly large Year 11 boy decided to push him back.

Darren was thrown backwards against the opposite wall of the corridor. He was winded and a little shaken, but otherwise uninjured.

"Can't you see what you've just done?" the older boy shouted at Darren. Darren had no idea what he was talking about at first, but then he noticed that the corridor was now silent except for the pained cries of a girl.

In his haste to get to his lesson, he had knocked over a Year 7 girl. She had been unable to get to her feet in all the confusion and had been trampled by those around her as they struggled to regain their balance after Darren had barged through them.

The girl continued to lie on the floor, her face bloodied where she had been trodden on. In the shocked silence of the following seconds, Darren could see that her right foot was lying at a strange angle to the rest of her leg and she had started to shake from head to toe.

The next hour passed in a blur for Darren. He missed the lesson he had been so eager to get to as he spent it in the head's office being questioned about the incident. His punishment was manageable; a three-day suspension. What Darren could not cope with was the oppressive feeling of guilt. He felt physically sick at the extent of the girl's injuries and the knowledge that he was responsible for them. He would never forgive himself.

What do you think?

1. Describe what the corridors in your school are like between lessons. Do you feel safe?

2. Why might someone want to barge through others in a corridor?

3. Do you think the Year 11 boy was right to push Darren? Consider the potential consequences for Darren and those around him.

4. What do you think Darren's schoolmates will think of him after this incident? Explain your answer.

5. What do you think Darren's parents will say or do when they find out what he has done?

6. Do you think Darren's punishment is fair? Explain your answer.

7. Do you think Darren will change how he behaves in the corridors after this incident? Explain your answer.

8. Write a letter of apology from Darren to the girl he knocked over in the corridor.

9. Write a set of rules for students to follow during lesson changes to prevent problems in the corridors.

Fat?

The model in the magazine was stunning. She had prominent cheekbones and her collarbone stuck out a mile. There wasn't a ripple of fat anywhere and her legs were like matchsticks. Beautiful!

Oblivious to the hubbub of conversation and clattering cutlery in the dinner hall, Della turned over the page of her magazine. She heard her stomach rumble. It felt good. Mum had tried to make her eat breakfast that morning but had made the mistake of leaving her alone in the kitchen when she went to collect the post. It had only taken a couple of seconds for Della to spoon her cereal into the bin, taking care not to slop any up the inside of the bowl.

Mum had seemed so pleased at the sight of the empty bowl. She'd even given Della a big hug as she left for school that morning.

"Try and eat something, Della, come on," Della's mate Trin pleaded as she practically tried to spoon-feed her with a disgusting mash and gravy mixture. Just the sight of it made Della want to throw up.

"Thanks, Trin, but I'm really not hungry. Anyway, I still have a couple of pounds to lose if I'm going to look good on the beach this holiday." Della didn't want to hurt her friend's feelings but there was no way she was going to eat a forkful of fat.

"A couple of pounds? You've already lost a couple of stone! Why can't you see what you're doing to yourself?" Trin sounded angry. Della couldn't understand what she could have done to annoy her.

"What's your problem all of a sudden? You sound like my mother!" Della got up to leave. The light-headed feeling she had when she arose was something she was starting to get used to now. She left the hall so quickly she didn't see the hurt expression on Trin's face. She also missed the covert conversations on the teachers' dinner table as their beady eyes caught sight of her skeletal frame swamped by her school uniform as she left the hall.

Nausea threatened to overwhelm Della as she sat in her lesson after lunch with the sunshine pouring in through the window. She found that she couldn't concentrate on the teacher anymore; his voice was drowned out by the sound of her own heartbeat pounding in her ears. She was sweating and her vision started to close in. She tried to stand.

The next thing she heard was Mum's voice floating into her subconscious from what seemed like very far away.

"She's been refusing to eat much for about six months. She lost her appetite after her dad left. I thought she was just unsettled by him moving out, then I realised that she actually wanted to diet. But she's lost so much weight now that it's got to the stage where I don't know what to do anymore." Mum sounded as if she was crying. Della wondered why. She could hear the irritating beeping of machines and the hiss of an oxygen mask and suddenly became aware of the stinging pressure of a drip needle in her hand. The rate of the beeping increased with her rising panic. Her back felt sweaty and uncomfortable on the hard plastic-covered mattress but she was too exhausted to move.

"In cases like these, the parents often blame themselves, but the victims of anorexia can be very sneaky about not eating. They learn all sorts of tricks in order to deceive their loved ones into thinking that they are fine and eating well. Until, that is, the proof of a poor diet is there for all to see. Believe me, I've seen it all. I've known women who are unable to have children because of the damage they did to their bodies through not eating properly when they were younger. Anorexia doesn't just affect girls either. Recently we had a patient who had been bullied about his size and instead of seeking help, he decided to take matters into his own hands. He simply decided not to eat and became dangerously ill. He was in here for quite some time."

Della felt cross at her mum and the doctor for comparing her to these people, but she was unable to wake up properly and give her opinion. She was forced to listen to various accounts of cases of anorexia while they talked. They didn't seem to hear the beeping machine's increasingly rapid tune as she gradually fought to wake up. She had to endure stories about anorexic people causing irreparable damage to their own health, starving themselves to death even, because they wanted to be in total control of their body shapes. On and on it went until Della finally heard the scrape of chairs and Mum and the doctor getting up to go.

The word stayed with her, going round and round in her head. Anorexia.

Tears ran down the expressionless face of the seemingly sleeping form on the hospital bed. On the table in the corner of the room stood two empty plastic coffee cups above a bin full of tear-soaked tissues.

What do you think?

1. Describe what you know about anorexia.

2. What health and social issues can arise as a result of having anorexia?

3. Why do you think Della stopped wanting to eat?

4. Do you think Trin broached the subject with Della in the right way? Suggest other ways she could have expressed her concerns.

5. What do you think the staff at Della's school should have done when it became apparent that she was not eating properly and was losing a lot of weight?

6. How hard do you think it will be for Della to recover from anorexia? Explain what kind of help you think she'll need.

7. Do you think Della will welcome or reject attempts to help her recover? Explain your answer.

8. Do you feel that the media is in any way to blame for the importance society places on body image? Explain your answer.

9. Consider how men and women are encouraged to look in the media and wider society. Do you think these ideals are physically and emotionally healthy? Explain your answer.

10. Describe your own eating habits and experiences of dieting.

Sickly Sue

They won't notice, thought Sue to herself as she crept unseen into the girls' toilets after lunch.

It had been a lovely Christmas dinner and everyone had thoroughly enjoyed themselves during the best lunch break of the year. The school cooks had excelled themselves and the afternoon would pass for the majority in a sleepy haze of full stomachs and contented smiles as everyone looked forward to breaking up for Christmas at the end of the day.

As Sue had suspected, no-one questioned the reason for her late arrival at afternoon registration. Hardly anyone noticed her as she crept tight-lipped to her seat at the back of the classroom.

Breaking up for Christmas was quite an event at school, with the Christmas party and carol service taking place during the last week of term. But when the frantic pace of school life ended on the last day, there was always a hint of relief and an almost audible exhalation of breath from the teachers.

At the end of the day, the usual weary trudge home was replaced by an upbeat skip and chorus of light-hearted banter amongst the homeward-bound friends. The excitement grew with each step towards home. But Sue was very quiet.

"What's up?" Sinetta noticed that Sue wasn't quite herself and hung back to talk to her.

"Nothing, I'm fine." Sue managed a close-lipped smile and then, with her head down, broke into conversation to avoid any more questions about her wellbeing.

Good job Sinetta can talk incessantly about every topic under the sun, thought Sue. To Sue's relief, Sinetta had to go into town and left her at the bottom of the hill. Sue continued home alone.

Sue had grown accustomed to the dull ache and the growling rumbles in her stomach. It had been going on for nearly a year now and she'd got away with it so far without anyone noticing. She knew it was wrong to binge on food and then purge it from her system when the guilt of having an overstuffed stomach engulfed her. She knew it was not doing her health any good. She just found it impossible to stop.

This unexpected development could change everything. This was something she had not expected. This was something she could not hide.

It had all started with a throwaway comment from Jamila about her weight. They had never been friends and Jamila seemed to go out of her way to be rude to her. Sue had never let anything she said bother her before though. She had tolerated Jamila's comments about her hair colour, her dad being out of work and the fact she didn't have the latest gadgets. They had been forced into an emotional box labelled 'Comments Made by Ignorant People' and the lid firmly slammed shut.

However, Sue had been painfully conscious of her changing shape and had felt fat and clumsy at the time. Her favourite clothes had no longer fit over her growing hips and increasing chest measurements. It was bad timing for Jamila's comment. Sue hated herself more and more as time went by.

Her weight had dropped a couple of kilos but, as she was growing taller anyway, her mum had just presumed that she couldn't grow up and out at the same time. Sue had also taken to wearing baggy clothing to make her weight loss less evident. Mum couldn't see what was going on. Sue had learnt all sorts of tricks to hide her secret, but she wouldn't be able to hide this. It was too obvious.

The dentist had noticed her teeth weakening last month. He had tried to warn her without openly saying what he suspected, but she hadn't taken any notice. Now this.

Letting herself into the house, she was relieved that her mum wasn't home yet and walked up the stairs as fast as her tired body could take her. She sat on the bed, exhausted, weeping silent tears as she looked down at the near transparent portion of her front tooth lying in the palm of her hand. It had snapped off in her mouth as she was trying to swill out the acidic bitterness of vomit. She felt such a mess. If only she had heeded the warnings of her dentist. He had told her that stomach acid eroded tooth enamel. He had even given her a mirror so she could see the damage that she had already done to the back of her front teeth. His warning had been too late.

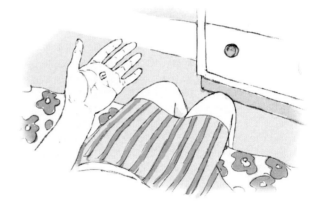

What do you think?

1. What do you know about the condition Sue suffers from? List the emotional and physical effects it can have.

2. How does bulimia differ from anorexia?

3. Explain what is meant by the words 'binge' and 'purge' in relation to this story.

4. Who do you think could help Sue with the way she feels about her body?

5. What could you do or say to help a friend suffering from an eating disorder? Consider whether your actions would depend on whether or not they'd asked for help.

6. What do you think Sue could do to overcome her problems and start to improve her health?

7. How do you think Sue should have dealt with Jamila's comments?

8. If someone said something cruel and personal to you, how would it affect you? Draw on personal experience when answering if you can.

9. Why do you think some people choose to say cruel things to or about others?

10. Write a short script of the conversation that you think Sue should have with her mum when she returns home. Remember that her mum is unaware of what has been happening until this moment.

I feel such a fool

"I don't want to talk about it!" Martine was starting to lose it now. Her mate Abbie should learn to keep her mouth shut!

"They say the truth hurts. Admit it, you should have listened to me. I warned you, but did you listen? No, you—" Abbie noticed Martine's face and finally got the message. "Okay, I'm sorry, I was just saying..." As her voice trailed off, Martine sighed.

"Look, I'm sorry too. I just feel a bit raw." Martine sounded totally defeated. She knew Abbie was right. She knew she should have listened. But she had let her pride get the better of her. She had hoped that she could look good in front of the other girls by having a boyfriend to show off. How stupid that seemed now!

Abbie went to sit by her friend. She was glad she had come to see Martine. She didn't have the heart to tell her everything that had been said in school, but at least she could reassure her friend that she was there for her.

"So, come on, tell me all about it. It can't be that bad, can it?" Abbie's coaxing voice was soft and Martine looked sideways at her with unreadable eyes. She looked away again to stare at the soggy tissue in her clenched fist.

"You know I told you ages ago about the way Stella's gang used to treat me in primary school? The three of them were horrible. Even now, if I close my eyes, I can still hear their chants and laughs at my expense. I hated it. I know I should have told someone but it was easier not to. I wasn't strong enough to deal with the repercussions. Well, I thought everything was okay now we're in secondary school. They're not in any of my classes and they actually seemed okay in the corridor if we passed each other. Stella even smiled at me a few weeks back." Martine blew her nose into her disintegrating tissue and threw it into the bin in the corner of her bedroom.

"Anyway, I only had my Facebook account to keep in touch with Dad, you and Tina. When Stella sent me a friend request I didn't know what to do. I didn't want to accept her but I thought that if I didn't, she would cause trouble for me in school again. So I did and apart from a few silly comments at first, she didn't have a lot to say and I'd heard nothing since then." Abbie noticed that Martine's voice was shaking slightly and she got her another tissue, just in case. Martine continued.

"So like I told you, Gary sent me the friend request last week. He didn't have a picture or anything but he sounded great. He said he was new to the area and had just sent out some random friend requests to people in the hope of making new friends. I just accepted what he said without thinking. We messaged each other a few times and he sounded perfect. You said he sounded *too* perfect. I knew you were trying to warn me so I stopped telling you anything about him. It was easier to tell you I'd blocked him. But I hadn't. He told me all about himself and he said such sweet things to me. When he asked to meet up I jumped at the chance. I felt like I already knew him, so what was the harm?"

Martine stayed quiet for a long time, deep in thought. Abbie sat quietly by her side, not wanting to talk in case Martine clammed up again.

"Well, I agreed to meet him at a party he was having at his house. He told me not to take anyone with me because his dad had invited all his friends and the place was too small to invite too many. I just didn't think. I didn't mention it to you because I'd told you I'd blocked him." Martine started to cry. Abbie placed her hand on her shoulder and waited for her tears to subside. With a big sniff, Martine was able to continue once more.

"I arrived at the address Gary had given me. It was a pokey little flat and there was no sound of a party coming from it. Why didn't I walk away? Why did I ring the doorbell?" With another shuddering sob, Martine dissolved into tears again. Abbie was almost crying with her.

"This scruffy bloke answered the door with a cigarette in his mouth and his hair stuck up at all angles. He stank. Then I heard that familiar laugh. There was Stella in the back of the room nearly wetting herself with laughter! Then suddenly the other two jumped out from the side and took a photo of me standing there by him." Martine was clenching and unclenching her fists, her voice broken with emotion. "That's the photo that Stella posted on her wall and everyone's seen now. Everyone thinks he's my boyfriend!"

Abbie wanted to tell her friend how much worse it could have been, that anything could have happened to her. She decided now was not the time.

As Martine rocked to and fro, sobs jolting her body and tears streaming down her face, one coherent comment burst from her.

"I feel such a fool!"

What do you think?

1. Why do you think social media sites are so popular?

2. List some advantages and disadvantages of using social media sites.

3. Would you accept someone you didn't particularly like or know as a friend on Facebook? Explain your answer.

4. What concerns would you have about meeting someone for the first time after talking to them on a social media site? Suggest how you could protect yourself.

5. If Martine had sought help in primary school about the problems she was having with Stella, do you think things could have been different for her in secondary school? Explain your answer.

6. Martine knows that the photograph of her and Gary has gone public online. Find out what could be done to erase the photo.

7. Why do you think Martine wanted to have a boyfriend?

8. If Abbie was your friend, would you welcome her advice or would you be irritated by it? Explain your answer.

9. *It is easier to bully someone over social media than face to face.*
    Do you agree with this statement? Explain your answer.

10. Write an ending for this story in which Martine returns to school.
    Consider the following:

    - what has happened to Stella and her friends, if anything
    - what other people already know, or think they know, about the incident
    - what other students say to Martine
    - how Martine reacts to any comments
    - whether or not Martine chooses to report the incident.

Is it just me?

"Layla? How was school?" Mum called from the kitchen as she heard the front door slam and the muffled sound of a coat being hung up in the hallway. "Layla? Is that you?"

There was no reply.

Mum decided the rest of the washing up could wait and quickly dried her hands on the nearest tea towel before hurrying into the hallway. She found Layla sitting on the bottom stair.

"What on earth are you doing there? I thought I was hearing things when..." Mum's voice trailed off the moment Layla looked up. Her eyes were red-rimmed and watery, her face a mask of misery. Mum was horrified. "What's happened?"

"It's just me!" Layla stood up slowly and wiped her nose with a crumpled tissue. "I never fit in." She slouched past her mum and flopped onto a chair at the kitchen table. Mum followed her into the kitchen.

"Come on, love, please tell me what's happened." Mum waited while her daughter blew her nose.

"The other girls go on about boys all the time, Mum. They never talk about anything that interests me, it's boys or nothing! And some of the things they say are so crude; what they'd like to do with them, where they'd like it done and comments about boys' bits that would make you blush!"

"It's normal to be curious about the opposite sex at your age, love," Mum said gently. "Within reason, of course."

Layla rolled her eyes. Mum just didn't get it.

"I just don't feel that way about boys, even the ones in magazines and films that everyone raves about. I feel *nothing!*" Layla paused to look into her mum's unreadable eyes as they watched her expectantly. She was just going to have to spell it out. "Mum, I don't think I like boys!"

There! She'd said it! Layla moved swiftly on.

"Nobody knows how I feel. All the other girls are desperate to have boyfriends. They don't say as much, but it's pretty obvious from the way they talk. I want friends who talk about sport, gaming, books, films; anything but *boys!* Most boys in my class just annoy me, they're always messing about and being loud. I hate the way they brag about their girlfriends behind their backs too; they'll tell anyone who wants to listen what they've done with them. I bet it's all lies anyway, just to big themselves up in front of their mates!"

Mum sat quietly for a moment. "What are you trying to say, Layla?"

Layla sighed, defeated. Mum hadn't taken the hint. She replayed the scene from lunchtime in her head and tried to make sense of how she felt.

The moment she'd walked into the hall she'd seen Julianne and Blake, heads together, holding hands, eyes for nobody but each other. She'd got her lunch and chosen a table well away from their public display of affection. They'd been going out with each other for over a month and her best friend's behaviour was starting to sicken Layla.

Maxine and Poppy had soon joined her and immediately started speculating on how far Julianne had gone with Blake. They had seemed to enjoy discussing their assumptions. Layla had been caught between wanting to defend her best friend out of love and loyalty and wanting to time-travel back to when she'd had Julianne all to herself.

Layla missed Julianne. She missed the way her face lit up when she smiled, the sound of her laughter, the scent of her hair, their conversations and secrets. Back then, nothing got in the way of them spending time together. Life hadn't been complicated by boys! There was no pressure to conform to what was considered normal, to fit in by talking about sex and things that she didn't fully understand. There was no pressure to have a boyfriend she would never fancy.

Mum interrupted her thoughts. "You like some boys. You like Simon. You two have been friends since you started primary school." Mum raised her hand to Layla's forthcoming interruption and continued unabated. "Yes, some boys brag and some are disrespectful but they're not all like that! I remember my first boyfriend. He was..."

Mum was in full flow. She still didn't get it. Perhaps she never would! Layla sat quietly, pretending to listen while her restless mind drifted back to lunchtime.

Lee and Mark had come over to their table and joined in discussing Julianne and Blake's relationship with Maxine and Poppy. Layla hadn't thought it possible for the conversation to sink any lower, but it did. She stayed quiet, trying to preserve her dignity by not getting involved. That was until Lee noticed how quiet she was.

"What's the matter with you?" Lee had asked her suddenly.

"Nothing! I'm fine!" Layla had responded snappily.

"You're obviously not. You've got a face like a smacked bum!" Lee snapped back. Despite the rumours about her, he still expected her to join in with what he saw as light-hearted banter.

Layla had put down her fork and taken a deep breath.

"I just don't like the way you're all talking about Julianne and Blake. It's disgusting!" The words were out before she could stop herself.

"Oh, really? You're just a stuck up, jealous little snob. We've all seen the way you look daggers at them. We've all heard what type of *friend* you wanted to be to Julianne!" Lee had stopped laughing now. He had stood up quickly, picked up his lunch and strode over to another table. Mark, Maxine and Poppy had soon joined him, grumpily kicking chairs out of the way as they went. They smirked and giggled and cast sly glances in her direction from their new table, sharing jokes at her expense. Layla had caught some of the horrible words they were using to describe 'her sort'.

Layla interrupted her mum's speech about her first boyfriend tearfully. "They called me names. They said I was sick, they said I was weird because I never join in with their banter. They said Julianne should have got rid of me a long time ago because of the things people were saying about us. They were saying things about me not fancying any of the boys, for being jealous and..." Layla dissolved into gasping sobs, her tears coursing down her face. "I just don't fit in!"

Mum hugged Layla and stroked her hair like she always used to, longing to keep her head buried in the sand where it had been firmly planted for the last few years. It was obvious that the hopeful reassurance that she'd always offered Layla in the past would no longer be enough.

What do you think?

1. How do you think Layla feels about Julianne now? Think about how their relationship has changed over time.

2. Do you think Layla reacted to Lee in the right way? Consider whether you think her reaction was justified and if you would have reacted differently.

3. If you had problems fitting in with the expectations of others, what would you do? Draw on personal experience when answering if you can.

4. What anxieties might someone have about tackling people who are bullying them?

5. If you needed to confide in someone, who would you turn to for help? Explain your answer.

6. Do you think Mum is really as unaware of how her daughter feels as Layla thinks she is? Explain your answer.

7. Do you think someone has to reach a certain age before they fully understand their own sexuality? Explain your answer.

8. Give your opinions on romantic relationships that develop in school.

9. How would you feel about a same-sex couple having a romantic relationship together? Explain your answer.

10. Consider how Mum might feel when she understands what Layla is trying to say. Write a script of the conversation that you think would follow her realisation.

She'll never know

"Mum won't know," Matthew muttered to himself as he switched on her laptop. As the machine whirred into action, Matthew could hardly contain his excitement. He quickly found Mum's password in her desk drawer and keyed it in. His mates at school had directed him to a new website. It sounded like a really good one.

With the start-up complete, Matthew connected to the search engine, typed in the name of the site and waited with baited breath for the images to appear in front of him.

What appeared was better than he could have imagined. The site was everything his mates had told him and more. He didn't even need to register to get the most hardcore images he had ever seen. The website catered for all sorts of fantasies and before long he had totally lost himself in the world of pornography.

Eventually, Matthew put everything back where he had found it, switched off his mum's laptop and crept downstairs to put the kettle on. He just hoped he wouldn't look so guilty when Mum returned from shopping that he'd give himself away.

Matthew's Saturday morning exploits became a regular event from then on. Mum never found out and in time he became more adventurous, hunting out sites that satisfied his curiosity and then passing on information about them to his mates so they could tune in too.

Some of the material was sick, but Matthew wasn't doing any harm. He was just a typical curious teenage boy, wasn't he?

A few months later, Matthew had a history assignment to complete by fourth lesson the following day and was about to make a start on it. He happened to glance into his mum's open bedroom door as he passed it on his way to his room. He stopped, horrified.

"Mum!" Matthew shouted down the stairs as loud as he could.

"What's the matter?" Mum shouted back, running to the bottom of the stairs. "Are you okay?"

"Yeah! I just wondered where your laptop's gone?"

"Is that all? I thought you were hurt or something. It developed a fault this morning; it messed up all my appointments. I had to go into the office to report it and now it's being mended." Mum returned to the kitchen to finish making dinner.

Upstairs, Matthew's mind was in turmoil. He'd forgotten his mum only had the laptop because her company had given it to her for when she worked from home. Who was repairing it? What if they saw the internet browsing history? Would they blame Mum? Were the sites even legal? What about that one site he'd accessed by mistake that was really sick? Had he gone on sites that had infected the machine with a virus? Blind panic set in. He shut himself in his room, unable to concentrate on his history assignment, unable to think of anything but the hammering of his heart in his rib cage and the coiled snake in his guts twisting and turning into knots. What was he going to do?

When his mum called him downstairs for dinner, he felt sick and couldn't eat.

"What's wrong, love?" Mum asked, noticing that he'd left most of his food untouched.

"I've snacked a lot today. Sorry," he lied. He left the table before Mum could question him further. She didn't see him for the rest of the evening. She presumed he was doing homework and thought it best to leave him alone.

The following day, a miserable Matthew trudged up to his front door with his history teacher's words about how he 'lacked commitment' ringing in his ears. He had been given a detention for not doing his assignment. Just what he needed – more quiet time to worry about the laptop. Even his mates had noticed a difference in him.

Letting himself in, he realised that Mum was already home. She greeted him in the hallway, eyes red-rimmed and watery. She didn't shout; she didn't need to. The menace in her quiet voice was much more effective.

"Don't take your coat off, you're coming with me to see my boss. I think you have some explaining to do. It's either that or I lose my job!"

What do you think?

1. Why do you think Matthew wanted to access pornographic sites?

2. Would anything prevent you from visiting pornographic sites? Explain your answer.

3. Do you think internet service providers should do more to prevent access to pornography? Explain your answer.

4. Do you think that there is any harm in Matthew accessing pornography or that he is just being a curious teenager? Explain your answer.

5. Do you think Matthew's relationship with his mum will change after this incident? Explain your answer.

6. How do you think Matthew's behaviour has influenced his mum's relationship with her employers?

7. Consider the immediate and future repercussions for someone who is known to have accessed illegal pornography online.

8. Do you think pornography influences the way that people view their romantic and sexual relationships? Explain your answer.

9. *Interest in pornographic material is fuelled by the media placing too much emphasis on sex.*

   Do you agree or disagree with this statement? Explain your answer.

What a life

It had been a hard day. Colin sat himself shakily on the edge of his bed, facing his mirrored wardrobe door. He caught sight of himself and quickly looked away. He hated what he saw.

He had known from an early age that he was different. As a child, he had never wanted his hair spiked up like the other boys and he had never liked being sent off to parties in jeans and t-shirts. He had wanted to be part of the boys' conversations, their games of footie and their rough and tumble antics, but he also enjoyed the feel of girl's clothes and loved their party costumes with their sparkly princess satin and colourful fairy netting.

Colin had felt stressed all day. His job meant that he was always on the go, always meeting people, always having to meet targets. His inner turmoil, the guilt and frustration he felt, only added to his stress.

His relationship with Liz had started off well. In the beginning she had been very understanding. But the novelty had unsurprisingly worn thin over the last six months and he had found himself alone once more following a blazing row last week. Colin knew that he could never expect a woman to fully understand his own preference for women's clothing. He could never expect a woman to understand how suffocated he felt on a daily basis in his business suits and his stiff, starchy collar and tie. The pressure of his daily pretence of happiness was getting worse the older he got.

He may have money in the bank, a big car, a lovely house and all the trappings of a successful existence, but what was the point of all that when he felt so isolated inside?

Now this!

His reflection seemed to beckon him to look at it again. His eyes were drawn to the image that awaited him. He sat unblinking for what seemed an eternity, looking deep into the eyes of his other self.

The blood from the cut above his left eye had run its course in rivulets down the side of his cheek. He spotted the false eyelashes missing from his half-closed eye clinging to the front of his dress like a spider. His laddered tights revealed grazed knees covered in gravel. What a sight.

For the first time ever, Colin cried. Tears of pain and anger? Tears of frustration and shame? He couldn't tell. He cried as if his heart would break and realised suddenly that he was afraid. Afraid that they knew where he lived. Afraid that his boss would find out and he would lose his job. Afraid to be himself.

What do you think?

1. What is meant by the word 'transgender'?

2. Describe your opinion of Colin with regard to his desire to dress up as a woman.

3. Imagine that a friend of yours wanted to dress up in a way that would mark them out as 'different'. Explain how you would react to this and whether you think it would alter your relationship.

4. Consider whether or not you find it easy to accept others' differences. Are there any differences you think you'd find it hard to accept? Explain your answer.

5. If you saw a transgender person in the street, how would you react? Consider whether or not your behaviour would be different if you were with a group of friends or on your own at the time.

6. What do you think has happened to Colin? Describe the type of people you imagine to be responsible for his current situation.

7. If you were Colin, what would you do to try to move on with your life after this incident?

8. Colin seems to feel depressed, ashamed and guilty about the way he is. Give your views on his opinion of himself.

9. How do you think Colin's life would change if his employers discovered his preference for women's clothing?

10. Can you understand why Colin's ex-girlfriend found it hard to be in a relationship with him? Explain your answer.

Who does he think he is?

Mr Bennett was a supply teacher. He was very good at his job and in his previous school, he had been a valued member of staff, well-liked by teachers and students alike. He had left his old job when he had moved house and had not been at his new school for long. He had been full of enthusiasm when he had started, despite having to cope with the stress of moving at the same time. He was, after all, a professional, and did not believe that anything that troubled him at home should have an impact on his working life. But now, sat in the headteacher's office, that enthusiasm seemed a dim and distant memory.

It had not taken Class 9d long to grind him down. During his lessons, the students showed little regard for his feelings and no respect for him as their teacher. They often refused to do what he asked.

"Who does he think he is? He's not our teacher!" they would mumble sulkily to one another as soon as he started to deliver a lesson.

He had to cover their lessons every time their usual teacher was away and it was always the same. Most of the class were noisy, disruptive and would do nothing that was asked of them. He tried to teach the few that were trying to listen and take part fully, but despite handing out numerous detentions and punishments to the rest, he was troubled by the feeling that he was failing the hard-working minority in the class.

After six months it had reached the point where the students would not acknowledge him whenever they saw him in the corridor, preferring instead to smirk to one another or nudge each other knowingly. Mr Bennett often heard mumbled expletives concerning himself as he passed, but chose to rise above it and ignore them. Besides, punishments were having little effect; the students seemed almost proud to get them.

That morning, everything had come to a head. Mr Bennett had had enough.

Class 9d's teacher Mr Hobbs was away again, and it was likely that he would be for some time. It was up to Mr Bennett to step in at short notice as he was the only one available to cover the lessons for an extended period of time. Before he had become ill, Mr Hobbs had started preparing them for their end-of-year assessment tests, a task which Mr Bennett would now have to finish.

As Mr Bennett had entered the class that morning, there was a collective sigh from the assembled students followed by silence in response to his cheery 'Good morning!'.

"Turn to page 65 of your textbooks and write today's date in your exercise books, please," Mr Bennett had asked politely.

"Why should we, sir? Who do you think you are? You can't make us, you're not our teacher!" Sonny, the classroom joker, had been quick to reply. Others caught on and also refused to do what was asked. Mr Bennett was left standing nervously at the front of the classroom. All his energy had suddenly left his body and he had found himself sinking into his seat, dejected and exhausted.

The class had watched as he put his head in his hands for a few moments before quietly leaving the classroom. For once, they were silent.

What do you think?

1. Why do you think Class 9d don't have any respect for Mr Bennett?

2. What makes you respect a teacher?

3. Why do you think Sonny stirred up trouble for Mr Bennett?

4. Do you think the others in the class would have behaved like this if Sonny hadn't done first? Explain your answer.

5. Why do you think that this kind of attitude sometimes exists amongst groups of students towards each other and their teachers?

6. Describe the effects of rowdy behaviour on the students in the class who want to do well.

7. Why do you think the students who want to listen to Mr Bennett don't say anything to the others?

8. Describe the consequences for Class 9d if Mr Bennett is unable to teach them while Mr Hobbs is away.

9. How do you think Mr Bennett will be able to gain more respect from the class if he returns?

10. How do you think the school should deal with Class 9d following this incident? Explain whether or not you think different punishments should be given to different members of the class.

If I could turn back the clock!

Trudging home after school in the oppressive humidity of summer, Esther could feel her trousers sticking to her legs and wished she'd thought to wear her skirt. The sun was beating down, warming the tarmac beneath the thin soles of her school shoes.

"Esther! Wait up!" Esther turned to see Sophia and Monique sauntering after her.

They're okay, Esther thought to herself. *Not exactly the type of friends Mum would approve of, but there's no harm in talking to them.*

Esther slowed down. As the girls approached, she could see the thick black mascara and sparkly eyeliner that they had applied after their last lesson without the headteacher catching them. They reeked of the strongest perfume Esther had ever smelt; it was almost making her eyes water.

"We're off to Jenkins' Chemist. We like the makeup in there. Want to come?" The girls looked eagerly at Esther, who saw no harm in a short detour. She knew that Mum wouldn't be home from work until half past five.

"Yeah, okay then." The three girls slowly made their way down the hill towards Jenkins', the small chemist in the centre of town. Esther remembered going in there for her prescriptions whenever she had been ill before the larger chain store chemists opened in town. Mr Jenkins was an old family friend, in his seventies but still working because it 'kept him young'.

The old-fashioned shop was cool and shaded inside and smelt of furniture polish and perfume. When the bell had stopped jangling above the door, Mr Jenkins shuffled out from the back room to see who had come in.

"Hello, Esther. I haven't seen you for ages! How are you? How's that mum of yours? I heard about the trouble with your dad. I was so sorry." Mr Jenkins seated himself behind his large wooden counter and obviously intended to remain there for some time.

The conversation rolled on and on and Esther actually found herself enjoying her chat with Mr Jenkins. He was a wealth of information and a real character. But Esther's attention was brought back to Sophia and Monique when she suddenly realised that they had gone very quiet. She couldn't see them, so she politely excused herself from Mr Jenkins and went towards the back of the shop to look for them.

When she found them, she was horrified. She took a moment to understand what was going on. Monique was holding open her school bag so Sophia could fill it to the brim with all manner of things, from cosmetics to first aid kits to shower gel. Anything that was within reach was being dumped into the bag. Sophia saw her and raised her finger to her lips with a quiet giggle, indicating that Esther should keep quiet. How could she?

"What's going on back there? What are you up to?"

Esther could hear Mr Jenkins shuffling wheezily towards them along the polished woodblock floor. He stopped when he saw them with a sharp intake of breath. Esther looked in turn from Mr Jenkins to Sophia and Monique. She was horrified.

"I don't believe you've done this. You were using me to distract Mr Jenkins! How could you?" Esther hissed angrily as she grabbed the bag and pushed the girls away from it. She glanced at the look of angry disbelief on Mr Jenkins' face.

"You wimp! We thought you were okay but you're just a wimpy mummy's girl. You stupid little nerd!" Monique flashed her a look of pure evil.

"We'll get you for this!" Sophia spat back at her over her shoulder as they left the shop.

Mr Jenkins turned to Esther. He had just realised what had happened.

"You don't need friends like that, Esther. Start putting those things back on the shelf while I call the police, will you? I'll call your mum too, the police will want to speak to you about all this." Mr Jenkins' usually kind eyes were hard despite his words, his manner and voice cold and professional. Esther wondered if he was acting differently towards her out of shock at what he had just witnessed. Then a terrible thought struck her. Did he think she was in on their plan? Would he ever see her in the same way as before? Was his trust in her broken forever?

Esther began to put everything back onto the shelves, all the time worrying about what would happen if she told the police the truth about Sophia and Monique. Esther wished she could turn back time and never have had anything to do with them.

What do you think?

1. What is meant by 'conscience'?

2. Why do you think Esther feels so guilty in this story when Sophia and Monique do not appear to have a conscience at all?

3. Do you think Esther would have felt any different if the shoplifting had taken place in a larger chain store? Explain your answer.

4. Would you have any sympathy with someone who shoplifts in any circumstances? Explain your answer.

5. Sophia tells Esther 'We'll get you for this!'. Do you think she will carry out her threat? Explain your answer.

6. What would you do if you were in Esther's situation?

7. Describe an incident where you or someone you know have been placed in an awkward position by those around you. How did you/they feel?

8. What would you do if you really wanted something in a shop that you could not afford?

9. In the story, it appears that Sophia and Monique were grabbing whatever they could, even items they didn't need. Why do you think they were taking them?

10. List some consequences you can think of for someone found guilty of stealing, including immediate and future repercussions.

I only did it to fit in

"I saw them do it. They wanted me to join in, so I did. That's it. I know it doesn't make it right but they made me do it. So what? It was only an old shed anyway. Other kids have had a go at it. It was covered in spray paint and there were bits of wood missing already. What's a bit more paint? It's probably only the paint holding it together!" Aaron started to laugh. Then he saw that the police officer was not amused and decided that laughing just then was perhaps not the best idea he'd ever had.

In the ensuing silence of the interview room, Aaron became aware of his mum sitting behind his right shoulder. He felt her tension and wanted to turn to look at her, but something stopped him.

"I repeat, why did you do it? Were you forced in some way to hold the can of paint?" The police officer kept his gaze firmly fixed on Aaron's eyes as if he was boring into his soul.

"No," Aaron eventually replied.

"So you chose to pick up the paint and spray it on the shed in Mr Williams' garden?" the police officer asked.

Aaron thought about his actions that afternoon. He had been bored so had decided to follow his brother Tom and his friends because they looked like they were planning something. He had followed them out of the house and down the street to the lane that ran along the back of the pensioners' bungalows. He had watched them stop at the back of Mr Williams' place and rummage about in a big rucksack Sean had been carrying.

Aaron remembered that a few weeks before, Mr Williams had called the police on Sean for terrorising his cat and Sean had not let the matter drop. He had been out for revenge. Aaron had watched as Sean had laughed and started to shake the can of spray paint. He had heard its metallic rattle. It was then that Tom had spotted him.

"Oi, Aaron! What are you doing? Spying on us? Go home!" Tom had said angrily, but before Aaron could turn to leave the scene, Sean had beckoned to him. Sean sprayed Aaron's name on the shed wall as he approached.

"Like it?" Sean asked. "Want a go?" He thrust the can into Aaron's hand.

Before he could stop himself, Aaron had sprayed a cartoon of his face beside his name to a chorus of gleeful shouts and cheers from Sean and his mates. But before he could hand the can back and run, Mr Williams had come out of his back door with his phone in his hand. He shouted at Aaron that the police were on their way. The game was up. Tom had stayed with Aaron while Sean and the others made a run for it.

Now, in the cold grey interview room, Aaron suddenly realised how much trouble he was in. He could still see the anger on frail old Mr Williams' face. Mr Williams, who his mum had often stopped to talk to in town and who had always had a £1 coin for him and his brother to go and buy sweets with when they were little. Mr Williams, who had only recently lost his wife. Mr Williams, whose only companion was the poor cat that Sean had been tormenting so much that Mr Williams had felt forced to call the police.

Aaron finally found his conscience, that little part of himself that he had buried to be tough enough to fit in with his older brother's mates.

What had he done?

"I'm sorry," Aaron mumbled, unable to make eye contact with the police officer. He felt dreadful.

What do you think?

1. Describe what is meant by the term 'peer pressure'. Who do you think is affected by peer pressure in this story?

2. Have you or someone you know ever been pressured into doing something you/they knew was wrong? Describe what happened.

3. Do you think the fact that Mr Williams' shed was already damaged makes Sean and Aaron's graffiti any more acceptable? Explain your answer.

4. Describe how you would feel and react if your property was damaged by someone joking around. Would your reaction be any different if it happened to an elderly family member?

5. Mr Williams is known to Aaron's family, especially his mum. Do you think this will affect how Mum and Mr Williams feel about the incident? Explain your answer.

6. Why do you think Tom stayed with Aaron rather than running off with his friends?

7. What is your opinion of Tom? Explain your answer.

8. Explain what you would advise Aaron and his brother Tom to do with regard to Sean and his friends. Would you have any concerns if you were in their position?

9. What punishments do you think the boys should receive from Mum and the police?

10. How do you think the boys should make it up to Mr Williams?

It's not so difficult

As the rest of the class quietly got on with the maths questions Mrs Rice had set them, Kurt sat at the front staring into space. His mind was full of worries. He couldn't do the work; it was too hard.

Everyone is ahead of me and they're going to leave me behind, he thought.

The longer he sat with his head down, the more worried he became. Tears cascaded down his face. His nose began to run and he felt silly despite the fact that no-one had seen him lose control of his emotions.

As his tears flowed, his stomach twisted itself into knots and his heart began to hammer in his chest. His breathing was coming in short gasps and he felt trapped, hot and uncomfortable. He didn't know what to do.

He looked down again at the question in the textbook. It just didn't make any sense. How could everyone else understand it? Why couldn't he?

"Kurt! Kurt?" Mrs Rice nudged him out of his thoughts with a gentle hand on his arm. "Kurt, are you alright? You look so unhappy and you haven't done any of the work. Can I help?" she asked quietly.

Kurt was so relieved. He spoke to Mrs Rice about his worries. She explained everything to him carefully so that he understood. She didn't make him feel silly. All he had to do was ask.

What do you think?

1. Have you ever felt that you were not as good at something as everyone else appeared to be? Explain how this made you feel.

2. How can feeling anxious affect someone physically and emotionally?

3. List some strategies that you think might help someone to cope when they are feeling anxious.

4. What do you think prevented Kurt from asking for help for so long?

5. What do you think could have happened if Mrs Rice had not asked Kurt what was wrong? Consider short-term and long-term consequences.

6. What advice would you give to Kurt if he had another problem like this in the future?

Turn the pressure down

It had always been easy for Charlie. She couldn't understand why the others constantly had their hands up in class to ask for help when everything seemed so simple to her.

Charlie had never quite fit in. Despite being bright, she had never boasted or put anyone down, yet the others were always making hurtful remarks at her expense. They pretended to be her friends; they were nice to her face but nasty behind her back. Never able to fully trust anyone, she had a horrible feeling that her classmates were jealous of her. Whenever she saw them talking excitedly about others, she was just glad that they weren't gossiping about her for a change.

By the time she left primary school she was bored and ready for new horizons. She couldn't wait for secondary school and the fresh challenges it would bring.

Her teachers at secondary school soon realised that she was very able and she was put in the top set for all her subjects. She even managed to make some genuine friends at last. Her family was so proud!

As time went by, the taunts of 'geek' and 'swot' went by the wayside and the pressure was on to do well and achieve her very best potential. No-one said anything to her, it was just a feeling she had. She had to be perfect, she had to get 100%, or she would fail herself.

After yet another poor night's sleep, Charlie rose blearily from her bed one morning to be confronted again by the multitude of worries and emotions that had filled her head the previous night. They were lying heavily on her shoulders and in her stomach. They were not just worries about success anymore, she was anxious about everything: what people thought of her, whether she looked nice, going out on her own. The list seemed endless. Her mind was almost hyperactive, always on the move over various topics, always having to think and be busy when she needed it to switch off and allow her to sleep.

Charlie couldn't face breakfast again this morning. Mum was worried; she had noticed the strain on her daughter's face. She chose not to say anything today.

The walk to school was more unpleasant than usual. Charlie's head felt heavy and her stomach grumbled its complaint to her all the way. Images blurred in her tired eyes and the headache that was never far away threatened to strike with full force.

She couldn't concentrate on anything during her morning lessons and found herself gazing out of the window on more than one occasion.

By lunchtime, the headache had struck. Charlie couldn't understand what was happening to her.

Another worry to add to the list, she thought sadly.

What do you think?

1. Describe what you think is at the root of Charlie's problems.

2. Suggest some short-term and long-term solutions to Charlie's problems.

3. Do you think any of Charlie's worries are justified? Explain your answer.

4. How do you think the people around Charlie could help her to develop more realistic expectations of herself?

5. What aspects of your life cause you the most anxiety? Describe how you try to cope.

6. Are there ever any occasions where it might benefit someone to place more pressure on themself than usual? Describe what they might be.

7. Describe how you feel when you are worried. Consider physical and emotional effects.

8. Who could you approach if you were worried about something?

9. Describe what you do to relax in your spare time. What else would you like to have the opportunity to do?

10. Write two paragraphs about what Charlie is doing in ten years' time. Write one for each of the following scenarios:

    a) as if Charlie has continued to put this much pressure on herself

    b) as if she has managed to overcome her anxieties and develop effective coping strategies.

What's wrong with her?

It had been about six months since Lily had moved away with her family. Her dad had been trying to get another job for months with no success, so he was thrilled when he had been offered the job in Cardiff. Her parents had thought the move would be good for them all; a fresh start.

It had been a sad day when Lily left. Jess and the rest of her class had made a big fuss of her and their form teacher had arranged for them all to sign a card and collected spare change to buy her a small leaving gift. Lily had been okay, just a little nervous at the thought of leaving to start again in a new school. She was really going to miss her friends too.

Life at school went on without her and only her close friends were still in touch.

"Did you get a text from Lily last night?" Miranda asked Jess one morning. "She seemed really strange. Nothing she said made sense."

Jess looked at her in alarm. "I've had a couple of messages like that. She usually sends them late at night. I assumed she was just tired. Maybe we should call her mum."

"I don't think she'd thank us for doing that. I'll call her tonight and see what's going on." Miranda and Jess went to their next lesson and put thoughts of Lily out of their minds for the time being.

That evening, Jess received a phone call from Lily's mobile. Lily's voice on the other end of the line was hardly recognisable. It was slurred and mumbling and didn't make any sense. Jess was worried and told her mum, who suggested she met Lily to see what was going on.

Two weeks later, sitting in the watery sunshine of late autumn on a damp park bench in Cardiff, Lily managed a smile for the first time in ages. Jess was horrified at her friend's appearance. Her once pretty face looked much older than the last time Jess had seen her. Lily had dark circles around her eyes and the spots and sores around her mouth added to a general impression of ill health.

"I must have sounded pretty stupid in my calls and texts," she said with a wry smile on her gaunt face. "But to be honest, I don't remember them clearly, I just remember a sad feeling. I needed to escape. Moving house, starting a new school, not having any friends nearby... it all just made me want to run away and hide."

Jess had been sitting with Lily for an hour. It was the first time she had been able to have a sensible conversation with her friend for a long time.

"You know that you're never alone. Why did you leave it until it got to that stage before talking to someone?" Jess paused to gauge her friend's reaction. "People at your new school

would have been approachable and understanding all along, you know that now. Don't you think you should have just opened up to someone instead of choosing to 'escape' that way?"

Lily sighed. She was so ashamed of having to admit to being so weak. She cast her mind back to the first day she was left alone in the house. She had found Mum's brandy in the kitchen cupboard. It was only ever used to make brandy sauce for the Christmas pudding. It hadn't even tasted very nice as it burned its way down the back of her throat and made her choke. That hadn't prevented her from finishing it off though. She'd been so ill she'd gone straight to bed. She'd told her mum the following day that there had been an accident, that the bottle had just slipped out of the cupboard and smashed but she'd cleaned it up straightaway, so not to worry! She'd hoped Mum would buy a new bottle, but she hadn't. Lily had wanted more. It had made her sleep properly for the first time in ages.

It wasn't long before she had stolen her first bottle from the corner shop, then another and another. The term 'downward spiral' sprang to Lily's mind and she smiled sadly at Jess.

"We're all wise after the event though, aren't we? I just felt out of my depth and very alone. But it wasn't the answer." Lily gave a shuddering sigh. "The stupid thing is that I never gave anyone a chance to get to know me. I've only now found out how nice they all are, but I've damaged my reputation and they just look at me with sympathy, like I'm unhinged. I don't think they see me as friend material now. I should never have done it."

Jess put her arm around Lily's shoulder. She felt sad that Lily's classmates might never know how good a friend she was.

What do you think?

1. Lily has been very unsettled by her family's move. Describe a situation you have experienced that has made you feel isolated or worried.

2. Do you have any sympathy with Lily over the way she dealt with her situation? Explain your answer.

3. What do you think makes someone feel the need to escape through something like alcohol?

4. If you felt anxious about something, how would you try to cope with your problems?

5. What do you know about the effects of alcohol and drugs on physical and mental wellbeing?

6. Do you think Lily's family will have noticed her behaviour? Explain your answer.

7. Describe how you think Jess and Miranda feel about Lily now. Do you think their friendship will have changed since she moved away?

8. Describe how you think the students in Lily's new school will view her now. How do you think this will affect Lily?

9. What advice would you give to Lily on how to move on from this?

10. How do you think Lily's friends, family and new school should have supported her through the move?

I'll show him

"So he thinks he can treat me like dirt, does he? He thinks he can call me names in front of his mates, does he?"

Selina had found a pin on the pavement on her way home from school and now, sitting in her bedroom, she drew it across the soft flesh of her forearm, pressing down hard as she went. She watched with satisfaction as the pin's point tore a ragged, beaded line of scarlet into her flesh. Only then did she feel released from the turmoil of her emotions. Only then could she relax.

When she felt calmer, Selina got one of her tissues from her bedside table and dabbed at the drops of blood escaping down her arm. It was one of her deeper cuts. Quite impressive, really. In the lamp light, she noticed for the first time the various criss-crossed lines etched in her skin, white against her normal skin tone, some as much as six inches in length. The more recent ones were still pink, but they would fade in time.

She couldn't remember when it had first started, but she knew she couldn't stop. She hated herself, so it seemed only right to have such little respect for her body. She wasn't even sure she wanted to stop; she liked the control it gave her, the feeling of pain and the release of all the emotions built up until that moment.

"Selina, come down for your dinner. It's going cold!" Mum's voice drifted up the stairs. Selina carefully put on a long-sleeved jumper to cover her arms, despite it being one of the warmest evenings for months. Mum would ask too many questions if she didn't hide her scars.

Things carried on as normal for Selina over the next few days. She avoided her ex-boyfriend and his mates and just stuck with her own friends around school. She tried to concentrate on her lessons, though there were times when the teacher could have been talking in Chinese for all the sense it made. Selina hated school.

© Rachel Adams 2015 *Stories with a message for the secondary school*   LDA   Permission to photocopy

On Friday morning, she woke up feeling a little sick. Her arm hurt. It had been itching around the last cut she'd made for a couple of days but now it was swollen and hot. There was a raised, red area around the scratch.

It must be infected, she thought to herself.

Selina tried to ignore the pain she was in all day at school. She felt terrible. Her temperature was up and nausea threatened to overwhelm her after lunch. She had to keep her jumper on to hide the damp patch on her shirt sleeve where the cut had started to weep. She'd also detected a nasty sour smell coming from her arm. She had sprayed her deodorant on her sleeve to try and mask it, but it didn't seem to help.

She didn't know how she got home. Every step sent pain through her head and arm. She was glad that no-one was in when she let herself in to the cool shade of the hallway. Selina dropped her bag and walked slowly up the stairs.

When she got to her room, she rolled up her sleeve and gasped.

"Oh God! I'm starting to rot!" she exclaimed with horror. The smell was horrible and the sight of her arm was no better. Yellow pus was oozing out of the cut and her fingers were swollen like sausages. Her flesh was an angry red and pain throbbed through it right up to her shoulder.

Selina was scared. She had never meant to do this to herself. What sort of scar would she be left with now?

She would have to get help. She would have to tell her family, but what would they say? As soon as she showed them they would see the other scars. They'd know what she'd been doing. The doctor would want to ask all about it too. The truth would have to come out.

The last thought Selina had before she lost consciousness was that this was one situation she would have no control over.

© Rachel Adams 2015   *Stories with a message for the secondary school*   LDA   Permission to photocopy

What do you think?

1. Why do you think some people hurt themselves on purpose?

2. What is your opinion of people who self-harm?

3. How would you feel if Selina was your close friend and you found out that she had been self-harming?

4. How do you think you could help Selina to understand the damage she is doing to herself and encourage her to stop?

5. Do you have any sympathy for Selina when she gets ill at the end of the story? Explain your answer.

6. Do you think Selina will self-harm again after this incident?

7. Do you think self-harming really makes someone feel better? Compare this to safer methods of dealing with anxiety.

8. List some problems that someone who self-harms might cause for themselves and those around them.

9. Consider how Selina might feel about her scars in the future in comparison to the way she feels about them at the start of the story.

10. Write a short story about someone who has harmed themselves. Include what made them do it and what the consequences were.

What a waste

A beautiful cloudless sky of bright blue hung over the landscape and the lush green vegetation stood out vividly against its backdrop. The scene before Josie from her hillside vantage point should have been soothing. It should have made her want to fill her lungs with deep breaths of fresh air and be grateful to be alive. But it didn't.

The ever-present twittering of birdsong retreated to her subconscious as the ceremony began. The deep, resonant tones of the black-frocked vicar sang their own melancholy tune in the graveyard in front of the audience of friends in school uniforms, teachers and relatives.

It was his funeral, yet Josie was unable to cry. She felt isolated, alone in this crowd of mourners. All of her friends were weeping silent tears, some were holding hands or hugging each other at the graveside, but she couldn't even shed a tear.

Will was selfish to have committed suicide. She hated him for it. That was that.

Josie watched his mum being held up by his dad. She didn't think he looked much better himself. She couldn't even begin to imagine how much they were both suffering because of Will. She saw his little brother, standing to the side with another relative, looking lost, trying to come to terms with life without the brother he adored.

How will he cope now? Josie wondered. *If Will could be here looking at all this, would he still have killed himself?* She doubted it somehow.

She and Will had been together for two years when she noticed a change in him. She was never possessive of his time and they both had their own groups of friends as well as their mutual crowd. But he'd started to hang around with the wrong gang. He stopped listening to her, he told her she was always nagging him. He even told her to shut up in front of his new 'friends' and they had egged him on. That had been the last straw. She had put up with so much by then that it wouldn't have taken much. She certainly wasn't going to be treated badly for his mates' entertainment. It was so disrespectful, so out of character for him.

He had been extremely talented. He was into sports, he was intelligent and doing well in school. His parents had started saving for him to go to university. He had wanted to become a doctor. There was nothing to stop him fulfilling his dream until he got in with that crowd, those idiots who thought it was okay to treat everyone like dirt, the ones who thought it was cool to take drugs and drink themselves into oblivion under the viaduct where they thought no-one could see them. He became an idiot too, getting into all sorts of trouble in school. His parents could do nothing.

She was glad she had been able to start talking to him again last year. He seemed to have come to his senses and had started to turn his life around. He was doing okay, catching up with his schoolwork, getting back in with his old friends. It had looked like he would be alright.

As the mourners all drifted away after the service, Josie walked down to a bench and sat quietly for a while. Her mum would be waiting for her outside the cemetery but she just needed a few moments alone. She hadn't been able to approach his family. She doubted they had seen her anyway. They were so dazed from the events of the last couple of weeks that they probably didn't know what planet they were on at the moment. She would visit them later in the week.

Right now, all she wanted to do was sit and remember. She remembered the happy times she and Will had shared when they had first met. She remembered him slipping on the ice when the pond had frozen over in the park, pulling her down on top of himself; his elaborate way of stealing his first kiss off her. They had walked for miles during the summer, discussing his dreams of becoming a doctor and his training for the annual sports competitions. He was so clever, so talented.

His old friends, his *real* friends, had told her he was never quite the same after all the drugs he'd taken; never quite as fast on the running track, never quite as carefree as before. Like her, they had tried to help him see sense when he first started hanging around with the new gang, but he had to *want* to get himself sorted out. No-one else could do it for him.

When he had finally realised what he was doing to himself he had tried to get his old life back. He had seemed fine on the surface, but he had so many issues that he couldn't cope with it all anymore. He had been a natural with his schoolwork but suddenly he was struggling to concentrate. He had once won sports competitions without really trying, but now he just felt pressure to win with a body that never felt as fit as it should. Josie realised that there was nothing more anyone could have done to prevent what had happened.

Josie finally found a use for the tissue she had been clutching all afternoon. Her tears were for the man she would never know. They were for his parents who would never know the pride they could have felt at their son's achievements and for his little brother who had lost his role model. They were for the way Will had ignored the help that was so readily available if only he had asked for it.

Her tears were for the tragic waste of what could have been.

What do you think?

1. Do you think Josie still had feelings for Will when he committed suicide? Explain your answer.

2. What advice would you give to Josie in order to help her get on with her life?

3. Will appears to have changed dramatically following his involvement with his new friends. What do you think might happen to those friends in the next ten years?

4. Why do you think Will wanted to die?

5. Describe what you know about the effects of drugs on mental health.

6. Could you understand someone wanting to take their own life? Consider what could make someone think that it was the only option.

7. Do you feel you could forgive a loved one for opting for suicide under any circumstances?

8. When a loved one dies, it can be hard to move on. Do you think it would be harder to cope with their death if they committed suicide? Explain your answer.

9. If your friend was behaving in a way that led you to believe they may take their own life, what would you do?

10. Research all the help that is available to anyone who might be contemplating suicide and design an informative poster to help people suffering from depression.

Grandad

Emily felt drained. They'd had a very early start to get to the funeral on time and very early starts are a particularly bad idea for a travel-sick teenager. The travel sickness pill had failed miserably, probably because she had been unable to eat something with it at such an unearthly hour before leaving the house. She had been so wrapped up in trying to stem the growing waves of nausea on the journey there that she had hardly given Grandad a thought. At least they were staying in a hotel overnight before the return journey tomorrow. She'd feel better then.

When Dad had first told her about Grandad, she had felt very little emotion. Even Dad just seemed a little shocked after the phone call from Grandad's neighbour. Mum had started to get a list together of all the people that needed to know and packed a bag for Dad so he could go there to 'sort things out'. She was panicking that she might not be able to take time off work to accompany Dad and anyway, she'd need to 'look after the kids'. Emily's brother David had been out with his mates at the time.

Grandad had moved to the other side of the country after Nan had died and Emily remembered feeling back then that she was grieving the loss of two grandparents, not just one. Grandad had moved so soon after Nan's funeral that even Dad was hurt. Emily was ten at the time but she remembered it as if it was yesterday. She particularly remembered the removal men in their big lorry, crammed full of her grandparents' treasured possessions that had been so familiar to her when she was a little girl. She had waved Grandad off as he followed the lorry in his car, feeling hurt and upset. Since then they had only seen him a few times at Christmas or during the summer holidays. It had been very different when Nan was alive and they'd lived so much closer.

Emily remembered that when she was little her family didn't have a car, so they had relied on Grandad for adventures that would take them further afield. Back then, they usually walked everywhere – to school, to town, to clubs and activities at the weekends. It was during the holidays that Grandad sprang into action as Super-Gramps. He and Nan would pull up outside their house and toot the horn of their huge car three times. Mum and Dad would have prepared a picnic and Emily and her brother would race each other to the car with Mum shouting 'Mind the road!' after them.

Emily remembered many day trips and summer holidays spent with Nan and Grandad. Nan was soft and cuddly and full of chatter. Grandad was always the quiet, serious driver who tolerated the noise of the young rather than relished it. He liked a quiet life but was always quick to accept a hug or a kiss on the cheek from his grandchildren.

Back at the hotel after the funeral, Emily realised how sad she was at Grandad's passing. The funeral had made her remember all the times that she had spent with him when she was younger.

She supposed it had been what people would call a 'nice' funeral. Lots of family and the new friends he had made after he had moved house were there. They had all seemed to care about him. She had cried at his funeral but now, alone at last in her impersonal hotel room, she realised that she had been crying partly because her mum and dad had cried. Even her brother had shed a tear. She had cried for the Super-Gramps she had known when she was younger, the one who had been happy to chauffeur them around and take them on adventures, not the one she had lost after Nan's funeral when he moved away without a second thought for them.

The man he became in later years was almost a stranger to her. They no longer enjoyed doing the same things together. The last time she had seen him, he had spent most of his time engrossed in the newspaper and asking for cups of tea. The reality was that she hadn't really known him anymore. Emily guessed that she had already grieved for him once before, a long time ago, and she had spent today merely paying her respects. Emily didn't feel guilty about that. Why should she?

What do you think?

1. Emily felt that she was 'merely paying her respects' to her grandad at his funeral. What do you think she means by this?

2. How do you think paying your respects at a funeral differs from grieving?

3. Give your opinion about Emily's reaction to her grandad's death.

4. Why do you think someone might want to go to a funeral if they feel very little for the person who has died?

5. Explain how you think Emily feels about her nan's death. Do you think she has come to terms with it yet?

6. Why do you think Grandad wanted to move so quickly after Nan's death? Explain whether or not you think he was right to do so.

7. Do you think Emily will need any support with the way she is feeling about her grandad? Explain your answer.

8. How do you think Emily should try to support her dad following the loss of his father?

9. If you were struggling with the loss of a loved one, who would you feel able to turn to for support?

10. What support do you think your school should give to students who have lost a loved one?

He's gone

"I sometimes forget that Dad's gone. He died a while ago now but sometimes it feels like yesterday. We used to watch the footie together and go to the park on Sunday afternoons for a kickabout. I liked that. He always made life seem fun. It's different now. Mum's always busy doing housework or cooking or she's out working. She's never in the mood for a laugh." Pat took a swig from his beer can before passing it to Matty.

"Mum hates football. She hasn't got a clue who plays for who. Useless." Pat took the can back and took another mouthful. Matty didn't interrupt. It was clear his friend needed to talk and have someone just listen, today of all days.

Pat continued. "Sometimes Dad and I would go to watch a match down at the stadium and he'd get me a burger. I really miss that. Mum hasn't got the money and if she did, she wouldn't want to go. She'd be too scared to let me go on my own too. She's so protective now, it's a wonder she let me out of the house to meet you this morning!"

Pat squashed the empty can in his hand. He seemed satisfied with his show of strength and threw it into the bin beside their bench. He slumped forward to rest his elbows on his knees and watched the clouds skim the tops of the distant mountains.

"Do you still miss him?" Matty asked eventually. Pat thought for a while and pulled out another can from the carrier bag by his feet. He opened it and took a deep swig of its thick foam before he answered.

"Yeah. But only when something reminds me he's gone. It's getting easier to forget, I suppose."

Pat sat up slightly and pulled his hood up over his head to keep warm. It was bitterly cold and Matty was starting to shiver. He was desperate to go home but he couldn't leave Pat in this state. They'd been friends since primary school and had been through a lot together. Pat had been there for him when his parents had got divorced. Pat had been there for him when he'd nearly got himself expelled from school. Pat had helped him to turn it all around for himself. Being there for his friend now was the least Matty could do, even if he was freezing his cheeks to the seat!

Pat offered him the can. Matty declined. He knew it wasn't the answer to Pat's problems.

"It's strange how things turn out. Your mum and dad hated each other and couldn't wait to part. My mum and dad loved each other and were desperate to stay together. Strange that, isn't it?" Pat's speech was starting to slur and he was swaying slightly in the wind assaulting the hillside.

"I can't believe it's been a whole year. He's missed so much already. Mum's changed, I've changed. Everything's changed. I hate it." Pat slopped his beer as he struggled to grab the empty carrier bag and flower wrappings from under the bench. He gathered the rubbish with his free hand, clutched it to his chest with one arm and stood up, swaying slightly, can in hand.

"Here's to you, Dad!" he said, finishing the remnants of his beer. He crushed the can and threw it into the bin with the rest of the rubbish. He stumbled and nearly fell into the bin himself before Matty grabbed him by his arm to steady him.

As he helped his friend out of the cemetery, Matty wondered what Pat's mum would say when she saw the state he was in. She had assumed they were just putting flowers on his dad's grave. Matty just hoped that on the first anniversary of his death, she would understand.

What do you think?

1. How well do you think Pat is coping with his dad's death? Explain your answer.

2. Do you think Pat has considered the impact of his dad's death on his mum? Explain your answer.

3. What impression do you get of Pat's relationship with his mum? Describe how you think it could be improved.

4. How do you think Pat's mum will react when she sees him return home drunk?

5. What reaction would you expect from your family if you went home drunk?

6. Do you think it is appropriate for Pat to drink beer in the cemetery? Explain your answer.

7. Why do you think that people sometimes turn to alcohol in certain situations?

8. List some of the potential short-term and long-term pros and cons of someone in Pat's situation turning to alcohol.

9. If you were worried about a friend who had lost a loved one, what could you do? Consider who you would go to in order to get advice.

10. Do you think Matty is a good friend to Pat? Explain your answer.

How dare the sun shine?

Dan trudged up the hill to school, his heart heavy. All around him, people were talking excitedly in small groups as they made their way to the same destination. No-one made eye contact with him as they passed him and no-one talked to him. Whether it was out of respect, sympathy or simply a misplaced fear that he would burst into tears and cause an awkward silence that they wouldn't know how to fill, he didn't know.

The sun was shining in the clear blue sky and birds were twittering in every tree he passed, yet it felt like his heart was being crushed in an icy hand that had refused to let go since that night. His desire for the world to stop turning was obviously not a realistic one.

Such a lot had happened since he'd sat his exams. He took in a sharp, shuddering breath as he remembered his mum waving him off to school the morning they started. She had her fingers crossed for him and was shouting 'Good luck!' down the garden path for all the neighbours, and probably everyone else in town, to hear. To say she was supportive was the understatement of the century! She always got so carried away.

Legs on autopilot and mind elsewhere, Dan hardly registered the warmth that was starting to colour his cheeks as he entered the school hall. Was it his imagination or did the general din quieten on his arrival? Was all attention on him for a split second?

"Hello, mate! Good to see you. How're you doing?" Caleb clapped him on the back with the force of a demolition ball. At least Caleb hadn't forgotten that he was still the same person he had always been. Since it had happened, only he had called Dan to see how he was, only he had seemed to care. Now, standing in the middle of the school hall, Dan could see the teachers' sympathetic eyes looking away from him. He could see that his friends didn't know what to say so took the easy option of averting their gaze.

Dan stood in front of Caleb listening to his rambling worries about what he'd do if he'd failed his exams. Dan had the feeling that he was only pretending to be subdued for his benefit, probably in some sort of misguided attempt to show respect. It was obvious that Caleb must be fit to burst with the excitement of the moment. He had waited for Dan to arrive before going to get his own results from Mr Baxter and Dan didn't feel it was fair to delay him any longer.

"Let's get it over with, then," Dan sighed, pulling Caleb over to the desk.

Dan watched patiently as Caleb ripped open his envelope, all the pent-up excitement bursting out of him in a deafening yell. He'd passed everything and he looked so proud.

Dan was pleased for him. Caleb urged Dan to open his envelope. He didn't really feel like bothering. He'd have preferred to take the envelope home with him and open it in private, but he didn't want to spoil the moment for Caleb.

An A in every subject.

Whoopee! thought Dan sarcastically to himself without the merest hint of a smile. Caleb was more excited than Dan, who just felt even sadder than he had before. He knew how proud his mum would have been, what a fuss she would have made.
All of his friends would have their parents to celebrate with that night.

As he stood alone, Dan could feel his eyes well up with tears that mustn't be allowed to fall. He could almost hear his father shout 'Boys don't cry!'. He knew he had to leave. He shouted goodbye to Caleb over his shoulder and quickly walked to the exit. He needed to be as far away as possible from all these happy, smiley people. He wanted to shout that they had no right to be laughing when he felt so desolate. He felt suffocated.

Arriving home an hour later, he was glad he'd taken the long route by the river in the park. There was nothing to get home for now. Dad was at the pub; it had become a second home since it had happened. He could tell by the loud music coming from his sister's room that she was probably crying. That was all she seemed to do these days. Home had become the disjointed dwelling place of three strangers, each suffering in their own isolation and failing to cope without Mum. No-one was able to open up about their feelings. No-one was able to talk about Mum anymore.

It would have been such a happy time if Mum was here. They would have celebrated somehow. Perhaps she would have cooked a special meal at home or planned a surprise meal out. She would have hung banners and balloons on the garden gate to congratulate him on his success. She would have bought him a 'well done' card weeks ago and would have subtly forgotten to give it to him if he had failed his exams. She always knew what to do, when to do it and how.

Instead, Dan found himself standing alone in a cold, lifeless kitchen amid yesterday's washing up and dirty laundry ready to go into the already overloaded washing machine.
He wished Mum was still there. If he could have stopped her from going out with her friends that night, the drink-driver would not have claimed her as his victim.

What do you think?

1. Dan notices how no-one wants to make eye contact with him or talk to him. Do you think you would find it difficult to know how to treat a grieving friend? Explain your answer.

2. Describe how a friend might feel if you avoided them because you didn't know what to say.

3. Dan appears to have lost interest in life. What do you think might help him and his family at this time?

4. Has anything ever made you feel how Dan feels in the story? Try to describe the circumstances and how you coped with them.

5. Dan and his family are struggling to cope in different ways. Explain whether or not you think their ways of coping are normal or healthy.

6. Describe the consequences that you think Dan's family may face if they continue grieving in this way.

7. In the story, Dan imagines his dad saying 'Boys don't cry!'. Describe what sort of man you think Dan's dad is and how his attitude might affect Dan and his sister.

8. Do you think Dan should approach his dad about being in the pub all the time? Consider when would be the best time for him to broach the subject.

9. Some people believe their loved ones go to another place following their deaths. What do you believe happens to people when they die?

10. Do you think that Dan's emotions are particularly strong because of the way in which his mum died? Explain your answer.

So brave

Walking up the familiar steps to Anna's house took Katy right back to her childhood. She had spent most of her summer holidays with Uncle Pete and Auntie Sian. Her cousin Anna was her own age and they were so similar they could be sisters. Putting down her suitcase, Katy rang the doorbell and waited patiently on the top step, wondering what Anna looked like now.

Mum had explained all about Anna's cancer and her desire to have Katy to stay over the Easter holidays, something she hadn't done for ages. They had lost touch after Katy and her family moved abroad when her dad got his new job. She had been ten years old at the time. Five years on, a lot had changed. Katy had been devastated to learn of Anna's ill health and had sent her a letter to wish her well. They had been writing to each other ever since. It had been lovely to receive the invitation and Katy hoped it would be just like old times.

The door opened.

"Hiya cuz! How're you doing?" Anna screeched excitedly and caught Katy in a bear hug.

"I'm fine, just a bit short of oxygen!" Katy managed to squeak. Anna let go.

"Come in! I hope you're hungry, Mum's cooked enough to feed an army!"

Katy followed Anna into the house. She couldn't take her eyes off Anna's thin frame and the back of her bald head, nor could she shake the image of her pale face, devoid of eyebrows and lashes.

Uncle Pete and Auntie Sian looked thinner and greyer than she remembered but they chatted non-stop over dinner, just like old times. They were amazed that she had travelled all the way from America on her own. They caught up on family news and Katy told them all about her new boyfriend back in the States. By the time they'd had Auntie Sian's speciality lemon meringue pie for dessert, Katy was suffering from jetlag and practically falling asleep at the table. She was sent off to bed in the spare room she had always used in the summers of her childhood. She fell asleep instantly.

The following day, Anna woke her up with a cup of tea and the news that her mum was dropping them off in town for some retail therapy. That sounded good to Katy.

Later, standing on the high street, Katy was impressed with the way Anna looked. She had put on false eyelashes and had expertly drawn on eyebrows with an eyebrow pencil. Her bald head was covered with a multi-coloured scarf that was tied at the side and she wore the latest fashions. Katy actually felt a little envious of her cousin's fashion sense and she told her as much. Anna just laughed and dragged her off to her favourite shop.

They talked for over an hour at lunch. Katy noticed how little Anna ate; no wonder she was so pale and thin.

They had planned to spend the afternoon in town as well but Anna placed her hand on Katy's arm just as they got up to leave.

"Do you mind if I call Mum to collect us? I feel quite tired now." Anna sounded disappointed. She had gone very pale.

"Of course I don't mind. We can do this again when you feel like it." Katy was too concerned about the sudden change in her cousin to care about shopping now.

Later, after Anna had taken herself to bed, Auntie Sian explained to Katy why Anna had been so desperate for her to come and stay. She said that the doctors had told Anna that her cancer was now too far advanced to cure and Anna had recently decided not to have any more chemotherapy. They thought she had about six months left to live. This would probably be the last time they would see each other.

Katy suddenly became aware of the ticking clock on the wall and her own heartbeat hammering audibly in her chest. She felt the heat of emotion rising up her neck and face as she fought to hold on to the tears that were threatening to fall.

Auntie Sian has so much dignity, she thought, *despite the fact that she must be going through such heartbreak.* Katy didn't feel she could cry in front of her; it wouldn't be right somehow. She saved her tears for when she went to bed and cried herself to sleep.

During the rest of the holiday, Katy respected the obvious fact that Anna didn't want to talk about her cancer and neither of them ever mentioned it.

Leaving at the end of her holiday knowing that this was the last time she would see Anna was the hardest thing Katy had ever done. It had been good to see her but everything was different after her chat with Auntie Sian. She realised that Anna wasn't just thin because she didn't eat enough, it was because of her illness. Her exhaustion was not because she wasn't getting to bed early enough, it was her cancer. Auntie Sian and Uncle Pete hadn't simply aged in the last five years, they were trying to come to terms with the terminal illness of their child and it was taking its toll on them. Katy had seen them watching their daughter with sad, worried eyes and it was heartbreaking. While Katy had been staying with them, Anna had never once let her bravery slip, remaining as positive as she had always been.

When a letter arrived at Katy's home in America seven months later telling her family of Anna's death, there was a separate thick, sealed envelope enclosed, addressed personally to Katy. Anna had written it just days before her death. It read:

> *Hiya cuz,*
>
> *If you're reading this, I suppose I must be dead! Don't worry, I promise I won't haunt you, though I might consider it if you get all morbid over this! I've had enough, that's all. What you need to remember is how much it meant to me to see you again. It was just like when we were both kids... great fun! I've told Mum not to tell you I'm dead before the funeral because I know how much a plane ticket costs and you'll only be in a state flying over here. I left strict instructions for her to write to you all enclosing this letter especially for you.*
>
> *I know what the funeral was like because I planned it, so I'll describe it to you. It was a celebration of my life. A bit different to the stuffy, all-dressed-in-black affair that Mum and Dad would have organised. Everyone was dressed in bright colours and brought loads of flowers. My favourite happy hymns from school were sung and Mum's lemon meringue pie was at the do after the funeral. I was cremated and my ashes were scattered down at the beach. We had such a laugh sunbathing down there before you moved away.*
>
> *Promise me that you'll enjoy your life and make the very best of it. Your boyfriend sounds pretty special, but don't tie yourself down in a serious relationship yet – live a little first. Oh help! I sound like Mum! On that worrying note I'd better get back to organising my funeral. Don't be sad for me. Remember me as the fun-loving idiot you loved to laugh with. I want that for you, not the weeping and wailing that some people think is necessary.*
>
> *Anyway, cuz, I suppose I'd better go now. Lots to arrange yet before I pop my clogs! Don't you dare cry reading this or the ghost of cousin-past will pop up out of your wastepaper bin when you least expect it.*
>
> *Love always,*
> *Anna*
> *xxxxx*
>
> *P.S. Hope you like my scarf, I thought you might like it to remember me by.*

Katy smiled through her tears and buried her face in the scarf that Anna had worn on the only day she had felt well enough to go shopping. It still smelt of her perfume. It would always remind Katy of the bravest girl she would ever know.

What do you think?

1. Give your opinion of Anna and the way she coped with her illness.

2. How do you think Anna felt when Katy visited, physically and emotionally?

3. How important do you think it was to Anna that Katy didn't know how she felt? Explain why she might not have wanted her to know.

4. What do you think you could do to support someone like Anna throughout their illness?

5. What do you know about cancer treatments and their side effects?

6. Do you think Anna made the right decision when she decided to stop having chemotherapy? Explain your answer.

7. How do you think terminal illness affects the family as a whole?

8. Do you feel that the death of a loved one following a long illness is easier to cope with than a sudden, unexpected death? Explain your answer.

9. In the story, two different types of funeral are mentioned: the 'all-dressed-in-black affair' and the 'celebration' that Anna had planned. Which type of funeral do you feel is the best to remember someone by? Explain your answer.

10. Anna mentions in her letter that she will be cremated and her ashes scattered at the beach. What opinions do you have regarding cremations and burials?

Beyond the doors

Ed couldn't believe it. He was in a daze as his mum's sobs drifted in and out of his subconscious, somewhere beyond the sound of his own wildly beating heart. His dad was pacing up and down in front of them, his shoes squeaking on the clinically clean hospital linoleum. The frown on Dad's face made deep furrows between his eyebrows and his eyes looked hollow. His mouth had become a thin line in his determination to make himself believe that this could not possibly be happening.

Down the corridor, a nurse laughed out loud. How dare she? To the Williams family, locked in their own private torment, the world beyond seemed selfish as it ambled through its mundane routine.

All thoughts were hijacked by the last forty minutes. All focus was on the double doors in front of the waiting area. Ed's imagination ran wild; he could almost hear the beeping of machines beyond, almost see the doctors working on his brother and feel the treatment that Stu was being subjected to. He imagined he was his brother, willing himself to survive, wake up, pull out his drip and rip off the wires monitoring his heart.

Come on Stu, stop larking around! You'll be okay! Ed thought he was going to go mad.

"I need a smoke. Sorry, love, I've got to go. I can't stand this!" Dad touched Mum on the shoulder and left without a backward glance. He hated hospitals and being without a cigarette had been torture for him.

Mum looked after him with resignation and gave a shuddering sigh in an attempt to control her tears. Silence once more resumed between mother and son.

The sight of the two police officers at their door before had been enough. They had not needed to speak; their sympathetic eyes had spoken volumes for them. They had asked if Mum was Mrs Williams and on her confirmation had immediately asked to come in. That's all it took for their world to be turned on its head. Mum had screamed and cried 'no' repeatedly when they told her, becoming increasingly hysterical until Dad had come in from the back garden to find out what the commotion was about. The police hadn't realised he was home and had to repeat the words again. They were no easier to hear the second time round.

"Your son Stuart has been involved in an accident. His motorbike collided with an articulated lorry on the A470 at approximately 7pm. He's been rushed to hospital by air ambulance but his condition is critical. We need to take you there as soon as possible." The words sounded cold and official. Words like that could not be delivered in any other way.

They were to the point, factual. There was nothing to give false hope. Shock had set in immediately.

Dad's squeaky footsteps announced his return. Unspeaking, he sat down heavily next to Mum on a hard plastic chair. Ed focused once more on the double doors still firmly shut in front of them.

Stu was bound to be okay. He was as tough as old boots. His leathers and his helmet would have protected him. He'd be fine, Ed knew he would.

The doors opened. A nurse rushed out, avoiding eye contact, and turned down the corridor. Dad stood up quickly and then sat down again in disappointment. Mum let out the breath she had held momentarily as the door had opened. Ed moved to the door to try to hear what was going on beyond and came face-to-face with a doctor as the door swung open again unexpectedly.

They were all asked to follow Dr Davies to his office. Ed knew somehow that this was not good. He could feel his stomach turn somersaults and his chest tighten. Pins and needles crept into his head, making him feel strange. He wanted to hear what the doctor had to say but at the same time he didn't. The doctor sat behind the desk and two other chairs remained for Ed's parents to sit on. Ed stood at the back of the small room, feeling faint.

The doctor said he was sorry, but Stu's injuries had been too extensive. They had done all they could but it had been too late to save him. Stu wouldn't have known anything about it; he had not regained consciousness. It would have been like falling asleep. The doctor said he was sorry again, and would they like a cup of tea? Was there someone he could call for them?

Ed stopped listening. His brother was dead. He couldn't be! He was too young to die, he had too much left to do. It wasn't supposed to be his time to go.

Amid his parents' erupting sobs, Ed quietly left the room.

What do you think?

1. Describe how you think receiving shocking news like this would make you feel, physically and emotionally.

2. If you were Ed, what would you do after leaving the doctor's office?

3. There are police investigations after a traffic accident to find out how it happened. How do you think this process will affect Ed and his family?

4. Do you think it is a good idea to see a loved one after they have died? Explain your answer.

5. Consider when you would expect Ed to return to school after his brother's death. How do you think he might feel at the prospect of returning to his old routine?

6. How do you think Ed's school could help him on his return?

7. Do you think some form of bereavement counselling would help Ed? Explain your answer.

8. What do you think Ed's friends could do to support him at this time?

9. How do you think Ed and his family will learn to cope without Stu?

10. What effects do you think the accident will have on the rest of Ed's life?

Time to forgive

Kyla heard Dad pick up the ringing phone downstairs and assumed that he would call her down to speak to her friend Heather. Or maybe Colin was going to pluck up the courage to finally ask her out – she knew he wanted to. She sat in her room listening to her dad's muffled conversation in the room below. He hated speaking on the phone but today he had no choice because Mum was out shopping.

She was surprised to hear the phone being replaced on the holder. She expected Dad to call up the stairs to tell her to put the plates to warm and lay the table in time for Mum getting back with dinner, but there was silence. Pity! She was starving. In fact, she was too hungry to do any more homework so decided to be nosey instead. Slamming her books shut, she rushed downstairs to see who had been on the phone.

"Dad, who was that? I thought it might be Mum saying she was bringing fish and—" Kyla stopped in her tracks. Dad was wiping his eyes.

"What's wrong, Dad? Who was that on the phone?" Kyla sat down by her dad on the sofa. "Mum's okay, isn't she?"

"Mum's fine, love. It's Uncle Greg. He's not very well. I'm next of kin, so the hospital has asked me to go and see him. He's really ill." Dad sniffed again. "You probably don't remember your Uncle Greg. We haven't spoken for years. I didn't even know he was ill."

Kyla did remember her uncle. She remembered the last time she had seen him too. Why did adults always assume that kids were oblivious to what was happening around them? She had been a lot younger at the time but she remembered the row. It had taken place in their garden after a barbecue during the hottest summer she could remember. The rest of the family had left and it was dark except for the glow of the dying embers on the barbecue. Uncle Greg had stayed to talk to Dad.

Kyla's bedroom window had backed onto the garden at the time and after she had been sent to bed she had spied on everyone outside. She had seen her grandad stumble down the doorstep and heard him telling her very disgruntled grandma 'I am sober, Muriel! I've been on lemonade all evening. Honestly!'. He hadn't, Kyla knew he hadn't! It was one of the funniest things she had ever seen and she had giggled about it to herself for a long time.

Uncle Greg and Dad had stayed outside talking while Mum did the washing up. Later, there had been shouting. Kyla had heard something about how Uncle Greg owed Dad enough money already without asking for more. Uncle Greg had hit Dad and Dad had fallen back against the barbecue. It tipped, spilling ash and cooling embers across the lawn before Mum could pull them apart. By then they were brawling on the grass like two schoolboys in a playground punch-up. At the time, Kyla had thought it was funny. Only later did she realise that they would probably never see Uncle Greg again. He never called Dad any more. He had tried to call her on her birthday later that year, but Dad had answered the phone and told him not to call again.

Kyla remembered seeing her uncle quite some time after the fight. She had been out with Mum in town and Mum's attempts to avoid him had been unsuccessful. He wouldn't tell her why he never came over anymore. Family occasions weren't the same without him, though. He was so much fun.

"They say he hasn't got much time left but I can't go, it's been too long. He wouldn't want to see me anyway," Dad muttered, seemingly to himself.

"Dad, who else will be with him if you're not? What if he dies all alone and you had the chance to see him but wouldn't?" Kyla was amazed at her bravery. For so many years, if Kyla had even mentioned Uncle Greg, Mum's almost imperceptible shake of the head and raised eyebrows warned her off. But Kyla couldn't bear to think of Uncle Greg being alone.

"I'll get your car keys and come with you. We'll leave Mum a note. You've got to go, Dad. This could be your last chance to put things right." Kyla wondered where all these wise words were coming from all of a sudden; this wasn't like her at all. It seemed to do the trick though.

"Alright, love. I'll get my shoes on," Dad said as he rose wearily from the sofa. Kyla scrabbled around for a pen and paper to write a note for Mum.

There was no traffic and they were at the hospital within half an hour. After a brief chat with the doctor they were taken into a side room where there was a figure lying in the bed. Kyla hardly recognised him as Uncle Greg. She remembered him as a giant with a typical rugby player's physique. He had had thick wiry hair and lots of it. The man in the bed was skeletal, attached to a monitor and drip. His hair was thin and patchy. She noticed with a start that he was awake and watching them as they each placed a chair at his bedside. The nurse was fussing about, talking in an overly loud voice as if he was deaf. At last she left them alone and Uncle Greg shakily removed his oxygen mask with one wasted hand. He coughed a wheezy, gasping cough and struggled to speak.

"I'm glad you came. I didn't think you would. Is this little Kyla?"

"Hello, Uncle Greg. It's good to see you…" Kyla's voice trailed off. It wasn't good to see him at all, not like this. Dad had been sitting very quietly by her side and she almost jumped when he spoke at last.

"Why didn't you tell me?" Dad had reached for his brother's hand and was holding it gently as if it might break. "We've been so stupid to have wasted all this time." He broke down. It was too much for Kyla.

"I'll go and wait outside, Uncle Greg. Love you!" She placed a kiss on his forehead, trying to ignore the cold, slimy feel of it on her lips, and hurried out of the room before her tears fell.

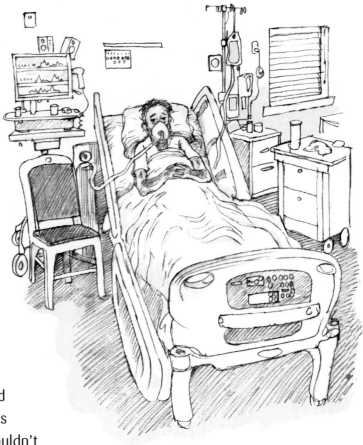

There was a small waiting area down the corridor and she shakily bought a can of cola from the vending machine. She had nearly finished it when there was a commotion coming from Uncle Greg's room. Kyla waited, slightly nauseous from the shock of the last hour.

A while later, Dad drifted towards her down the corridor, accompanied by a kind-faced nurse with eyes full of sympathy. He was pale, red-eyed and dazed and was clasping a small holdall full of his brother's belongings. Uncle Greg wouldn't be needing them anymore.

"Thank you, Kyla. I'm so glad I made it. We were just in time," Dad said quietly, avoiding eye contact as he thanked the nurse and continued towards the exit. Kyla quietly followed, her eyes swimming with tears, her mind fighting to remember happier memories of her uncle.

What do you think?

1. Kyla observes that adults assume that kids are 'oblivious' to what is happening around them. Are you familiar with this feeling? Describe when you have felt like this.

2. If you were in Kyla's position after her dad received the phonecall, what would you have said or done? Explain your answer.

3. Kyla lost touch with her Uncle Greg because of an argument between him and her dad. Do you think this was fair on Kyla? Explain your answer.

4. How do you think the adults in the story could have dealt with the argument differently?

5. Why do you think the dispute between Uncle Greg and Kyla's dad lasted so long?

6. Kyla helped to bring the two men together in the end. Why do you think her dad was so glad that he was able to see Greg when he seemed to have forgotten all about him in the years following the row?

7. How do you think Dad would have felt if he had not seen Uncle Greg before he died?

8. Uncle Greg chose not to tell any of his family that he was seriously ill earlier. How do you think he felt as he waited in hospital to see whether or not Kyla's dad would turn up to see him?

9. What emotions do you think Dad will feel following the death of his brother? Explain your answer.

10. Describe how you think Kyla will feel now that Uncle Greg, who had been cut out of her life for so long, has died.

They never knew

"Is there much in the paper, Mum?" Ben called from the kitchen as he made her a cup of tea. The sound of the kettle boiling drowned out her answer.

Since his dad had died, he had found himself feeling protective of his mum and called in on her most days before going home to his dog Buster. He had never met the right woman and failed miserably at relationships anyway, so he supposed he was destined to be a bachelor all his life. At least Buster was company to go home to at the end of another boring day at work.

Ben walked back to the living room and carefully placed the cup and saucer on the side table by his mum. She thanked him with a smile and went back to reading the local paper.

"Oh! Old Mr Millard has died!" Mum exclaimed. She was oblivious to the cold chill that suddenly ran the entire length of her son's body.

"Do you remember him? It says here that he died peacefully in his sleep after a short illness. He looked a lot older than seventy. Aw! Poor old thing. He was such an old gent. I bet he was a right charmer in his younger days. Oh, what a shame."

Ben watched as his mum continued to read the obituary pages and hoped that his face didn't betray his feelings. The room seemed to close in on top of him and he suddenly felt too hot.

"Mum, I've just remembered something, I just need to dash home. I'll call in tomorrow, okay?" Ben beat a hasty retreat and let himself out of his mum's bungalow, ignoring her questions as he shut the door behind himself.

Mr Millard: a name he had tried to blank from his memory, a name associated with a lifetime of hurt. He had never wanted to hear it again.

Mr Millard had appeared ancient all those years ago when he had walked his two dogs around the park as Ben and his mates had been playing football after school. The first time

Ben had spoken to him was when Will had kicked the ball out of play and Mr Millard had brought it back for them instead of kicking or throwing it. It had seemed an odd thing for him to do at the time, but he had gone on to be so chatty and kind to all the boys that they had assumed he just wanted some company. He had become a regular visitor to the park from then on.

Mr Millard had once been a councillor and was highly respected by everyone in town. He was known to be a good man, so when he had offered to help Ben with some geography homework he didn't understand, Mum didn't mind Ben going to see him.

Ben had set off and found the house after a short walk up Buckingham Avenue. It was big and detached and behind iron railings. Ben was immediately impressed.

Mr Millard had answered the door in shorts and shown Ben into his living room, where he had put books and an atlas on the table in readiness. Ben had been at the house for an hour and a half when he realised it was getting late. He had been so interested in what Mr Millard had been telling him about all the places he had visited that he had lost track of time. His homework done, he thanked Mr Millard and made his way home, happy in the knowledge that he was guaranteed a good mark for it. Mr Millard had turned out to be brilliant at almost everything and Ben found himself going to him for help with most of his schoolwork.

About three months after he had first met him, Ben was playing football in the park when he noticed Mr Millard watching him and his friends intently. At first he thought nothing of it, but it seemed that every time he left the house from then on he saw Mr Millard somewhere. Ben's friends noticed and started to tease him about his 'boyfriend' and eventually, too embarrassed to tell his parents, Ben had decided to go and see Mr Millard himself to ask him to leave him alone.

Buster bounded towards Ben as he let himself into his flat, barking and wagging his tale. He was a welcome distraction after the shock of hearing Mr Millard's name again. As he petted Buster on the sofa, Ben remembered the day he had confronted Mr Millard. It was a memory that had haunted him ever since.

At first, Mr Millard had been pleased to see him and offered him a glass of lemonade in the garden. Once he'd finished it, Ben asked him why he always seemed to see him around now. He told him that he was being teased by his friends. Mr Millard had become angry and accused him of 'leading him on'. He lunged at Ben and touched him inappropriately. Ben had been disgusted but powerless to stop him as the assault continued.

When it was over, Ben was in tears and Mr Millard became concerned, sorry even. He had let Ben go. Ben had run across his garden and vaulted the fence at the side before sprinting home to take the longest shower he had ever taken in his life.

Buster slept soundly as late afternoon turned to dusk. Ben was oblivious to the deepening darkness surrounding him as he remembered standing in the shower but not being able to feel clean. He remembered the shock of Mr Millard's touch, the bile rising in his throat over the next few years at the mere thought of that day.

His mind was occupied by the choices he had made. He had chosen to keep it secret. He had chosen not to confide in his friends and family for fear of ridicule or rebuke and by doing so had spent the last twelve years blaming himself, failing in relationships that could have brought him happiness and fighting depression. Mr Millard didn't deserve to die peacefully in his sleep as if he was innocent. He didn't deserve to have people thinking so highly of him. He should have been arrested for his crime all those years ago and made to feel the guilt and disgust that had weighed so heavily on Ben all these years.

But now it was too late. No-one had ever known the truth about him and now they never would.

What do you think?

1. Do you think you can tell by someone's appearance or general behaviour what they are like as a person? Consider whether Ben should have realised what Mr Millard's intentions were.

2. Do you think Ben could have protected himself from possible harm at any point in the story? Explain your answer.

3. How do you think Ben's personality and behaviour might have changed following his experience with Mr Millard?

4. List some possible consequences of Ben not telling anyone about what Mr Millard did to him when he was younger.

5. Who do you think Ben should have told about the assault at the time? Explain your answer.

6. List some reasons why you think Ben would have found it difficult to tell anyone about his attack.

7. Do you think Ben should tell someone about the attack now? Describe how you think they would react.

8. Who do you think could provide the right support for Ben now?

9. If one of your friends started going round to someone's house as Ben did with Mr Millard, what advice would you give to them?

Clumsy

"You must be so clumsy, you're always covered in bruises," Chris teased Laura. "Look at that one, it's a beauty!" Chris was pointing at a large purple and yellow swelling on Laura's shin as they sat together on the school field.

"That Trisha Bates is a monster with a hockey stick, she marked me out from the start of the match." Laura smiled weakly as she covered her shin with the bottom of her long skirt. She had been the butt of many jokes over her sudden preference for unfashionable long skirts and long-sleeved shirts. She had hurriedly bought them from the local charity shop last month. Normally so image-conscious, Laura felt like a different person these days.

Sitting on the sun-baked grass with Chris, feeling the warmth on her aching limbs, Laura felt something close to contentment. As Chris continued to talk non-stop about football, his dog's vet appointment and his mum's new diet, Laura almost forgot. Almost, but not quite.

She'd lived next door to Chris for years. They'd grown up together, gone to school together, had argued and laughed together in equal measure. His mum, Tracy, knew her mum too. They always used to be close friends, always calling around to each other's houses for a coffee and a chat. All that had stopped now. They only saw Tracy occasionally and she would ask how they were with concerned eyes, but that was it. Laura had never asked Chris about it and he didn't seem to have noticed the change in their mothers' friendship.

Laura rarely saw Chris outside school these days. He used to come round with his mum in the evenings or they'd all go to town together on a Saturday, but not now.

"Are you okay, Laura? You've gone really quiet." Chris was looking at her. The sight of his concerned face brought a lump to her throat. Should she tell him? She wanted to, but if she did, she was putting his life in danger. That was what Tyler had said. Within a month of moving in with her mum, he'd started to impose his will on them. Laura had distanced herself from her friends to protect them, making excuses to put them off coming to her house because Tyler told her to.

"I'm fine, just tired." Laura bit her lip, her eyes stinging with the sensation of imminent tears. Chris looked awkward suddenly, his hands pulling at tufts of grass. He looked at his watch. Satisfied that the thirty minutes left of lunch break would be sufficient, he decided the time had come. Laura watched him take a deep breath to compose himself.

"Are you really okay, Laura? Really?" Chris sensed her reluctance to talk. He and his mum could guess at what had been going on at Laura's house since Tyler moved in. The walls were so thin that they heard all the arguments. All the neighbours were talking about it.

© Rachel Adams 2015 *Stories with a message for the secondary school* LDA Permission to photocopy

The two friends sat together yet apart, isolated by their own thoughts. Eye contact was suddenly impossible.

The sun still shone, the birds still sang, groups of friends still sat chatting and laughing around the playing field, wishing lunchtime would never end. Yet something had started to change between Chris and Laura.

What do you think?

1. What do you think is happening in Laura's life at the moment that has made her change so much?

2. If someone was being violent or controlling towards you or someone you knew, what could you do to prevent the situation from continuing?

3. What sort of friends do you think Chris and his mum have been to Laura and her mum? Explain your answer.

4. In what ways do you think Chris and his mum could help Laura?

5. Would you expect the school to have noticed a change in Laura? Explain your answer.

6. If the school had noticed that Laura may be having problems at home, what would you expect them to do?

7. Do you think Laura's mum should have done something about the situation they are in now? Explain what you think she could do.

8. List some reasons that might explain why Laura's mum hasn't done anything about her current situation.

9. What difficulties do you think Chris may have trying to broach this subject with Laura? Write a script of the conversation you think they might have next.

10. Consider what you know about Tyler from the story and, using your imagination, write a description of him. Include his physical appearance and past behaviour.

Am I in trouble?

"We learned about 'stranger danger' back in primary school, but he stopped his car right by me and spoke as if he knew me, so I stopped to talk to him. I didn't actually know him but he said he knew my family. He told me he'd borrowed some of Dad's climbing equipment a few months ago and that it was in the boot of his car. He said it was lucky he'd recognised me as he drove past as he wanted to give the stuff back. When he got out of his car to get Dad's kit for me I just stood there waiting. How stupid of me."

Neil stopped. He picked up his plastic cup with a trembling hand and took a sip of water before continuing.

"Before he got to the back of his car to open the boot, he stood in front of me. I didn't like the look on his face. It freaked me out and I tried to step away from him but he grabbed me and held onto my arm, pushing against me to get me into his car."

Mum watched Neil as he sat in the police interview room. She was proud of her son; she knew how hard this must be for him.

"I didn't stand a chance. He pushed me hard in my stomach until I fell back into the car. He slammed the door and I couldn't open it – there must have been a child safety lock on it or something. I thought someone would hear me shouting but no-one came." Neil was shaking so much he could barely hold the cup in his hand. Mum looked at the police officer, hoping there would be no more questions after this. She encouraged Neil to continue with a reassuring nod.

"He got back into the car and drove off with me hitting the hell out of the back of his head. He just kept on driving, pushing me away with his hand. He drove us out of town and stopped by some trees, away from the main road. He climbed over into the back seat and started to—" Neil broke off. "He shouldn't have touched me. He shouldn't have done what he did. I couldn't stop him, he was too strong."

Neil couldn't talk any more. He was worried about upsetting his mum, he was worried about what people would say if they found out. Having to find the words to tell the police officer what had happened was so difficult because they were words he didn't want to say.

"I think he's told you enough, hasn't he?" Mum asked the police officer, seeing her son's discomfort. She was relieved to hear that they could go home now and that the police officer would call them tomorrow.

As they approached the car, Neil turned to his mum.

"Are you angry with me?"

She was surprised by the question and stood for a moment, key in hand, before opening the door. She struggled to find the right words.

"Of course I'm not angry with you. None of this is your fault. That man should never have forced you into his car or driven off with you or touched you the way he did." Mum found herself feeling very emotional. The last few hours had been so hard. She had been so upset and worried that she was surprised she hadn't broken down sooner.

"How could I be angry with you? You'll never know how proud of you I am. You've been so brave. Brave because you were able to get yourself home after the attack, brave for telling me, brave for telling the police, even though I could see how difficult that was for you." Tears were rolling openly down Mum's cheeks now and Neil placed a tissue into the palm of her hand.

"If you hadn't told the police what you know, there would be no way of catching that man before he does the same thing to someone else. If I'm angry with anyone, it's most definitely not you. Well done, love."

She was suddenly too emotional to speak so she threw her arms around her son and gave him a big hug. Despite being an image-conscious teenager with a reputation to uphold, Neil hugged her back, glad that he had told her what had happened.

What do you think?

1. Define the word 'paedophile'.

2. What do you think could have happened if Neil had not spoken of his attack? Consider possible consequences for himself and others.

3. What help and support do you think should be offered to Neil after his ordeal?

4. Why do you think Neil felt unsure about whether or not his mum was angry with him?

5. Do you think that what has happened to Neil will affect what he is allowed to do or what he wants to do on his own from now on? Explain your answer.

6. Have you ever been afraid to go out alone? If so, why?

7. Have you or someone you know ever been made to feel uncomfortable by what someone else has said or done? Describe what happened.

8. Do you feel that secondary schools do enough to ensure that their students are able to take responsibility for their own safety when they are not in school? Suggest ideas for other things you think they could do.

9. Describe what you could do to ensure your own safety when you are out alone or with friends.

10. Research websites and organisations offering advice to people who have suffered a violent or sexual attack. Design a poster to educate young adults about how to keep safe and what to do if they are attacked.

INDEX